NOT THE ONLY
TICKET

NOT THE ONLY

TICKET

An Autobiography

AARON MOLOCK

ARPress
ILLUMINATING IDEAS
EMPOWERING VOICES

ARPress
45 Dan Road Suite 5
Canton MA 02021

Hotline: 1(888) 821-0229
Fax: 1(508) 545-7580

Ordering Information:
Quantity sales. Special discounts are available on quantity purchases by corporations, associations, and others. For details, contact the publisher at the address above.

Printed in the United States of America.

ISBN-13:	Softcover	979-8-89356-735-9
	eBook	979-8-89356-736-6

Library of Congress Control Number: 2024908172

I dedicate this book to my brother, Louis Molock, who passed away in January 1983. He is the person I most respected in this world.

"Keep your face always toward the sunshine—and shadows will fall behind you."

~ Walt Whitman

TABLE OF CONTENTS

INTRODUCTION

I truly believe that everything that we do and everyone that we meet is put in our path for a purpose. There are no accidents; we're all teachers—if we're willing to pay attention to the lessons we learn, trust our positive instincts, and not be afraid to take risks or wait for some miracle to come knocking at our door.

~ MARLA GIBBS

Many people have desired to be professional athletes, but as they embark on the journey of life, it doesn't happen. I hold firmly to my conviction that I could have been an NBA player. Despite my eff orts to make that dream a reality, life, it seems, had other plans for me. I can testify from my own experiences that even if it is not in the cards for you to make it to the professional field, you can still be successful. No matter what you aspire to be, there is always a need for a backup plan.

I am not rich man, but, I have worked hard to be successful. I want athletes to understand that if you don't make it beyond a hobby, it is not the end of the world. I know your dream to become a professional athlete weighs heavily on you, but sometimes your purpose will take you down a diff erent road.

A lot of athletes are driven by the mantra, "If at first you don't succeed, try and try again." Very often, this thought process can keep us locked in a loop, an unending cycle of failure that keeps us grounded in our fantasy, hoping one day it will happen, miraculously. While I believe in miracles, we must be practical in our endeavors for success.

Many lessons are embroidered into the idea of failure, and we can learn from them. Sometimes success requires us to keep pushing in one particular direction until we fulfill our desires. On other occasions, we need to push in a different direction. Success requires flexibility and a whole lot of wisdom to know when to shift and try something else.

I learned many principles from my pursuit of the athletic dream, which I would like to call "Life Lessons." They became very useful in my drive to succeed. These I will share with you, interspersed with my own life story. You will see them throughout this book as little "Gems." These are basic identifying principles you may recognize in your own life, which points to change, development, and transition. Life is a series of lessons; if we pay attention and learn what we can, we will get the tools we need to be successful. We may focus on our failures and miss the invaluable nuggets they contain.

What is success, really? It is a byproduct of those who choose not to give up. It is a transmutational process where you learn what to do, and what not to do, allowing you to extract the principles you need to make life work for you.

This is my story, and it may not find a reasonable resolution in the end, because my story is still being written.

Chapter 1

THE BEGINNING

*Success is no accident. It is hard work. Perseverance,
learning, studying, sacrifice, and most of all, love
of what you are doing or learning to do.*

~ BELE

Everyone has dreams of what they would like to become. Society tells us we need to put one hundred and ten percent into pursuing our dreams, or we will not become successful. We all dream of becoming a professional athlete at some point in our lives, regardless of race. But what happens to those who give one hundred and ten percent and never see their dreams fulfilled because of the many obstacles?

 ALWAYS HAVE A DREAM, BECAUSE IT IS OUR DREAMS THAT DRIVES US.

When I was five years old, I dreamed of becoming a professional athlete. I had good coordination and I was very athletic. I loved three of the four major sports. I liked to play football and baseball, but basketball was my passion. I loved this game with all my heart.

 YOUR DREAM WILL ALWAYS BE IN LINE WITH YOUR PASSION. WHAT DO YOU LOVE TO DO?

Super Shooter

When I was nine years old, I often attended the Carroll Park Recreation Center, where I would meet one of the many Recreation Center attendants. One of them, Mr. Durant, convinced me to register for the Gino's Super Shooter Contest. I knew I was very good at basketball, but the thought of competing against other kids that I did not know terrified me. I was nervous even thinking about it.

The Gino's Super Shooter Contest starts at the Free Throw line and you are timed to make as many free throws as you can. You can also make layups, but you get more points for making the shot from the free throw line. There were ten kids in my age group. I made it through all the preliminary rounds and was scheduled to face off against a young white kid who was seven years old. Up to this point, I had the best score. In the Championship round, each contestant started with zero.

The young white kid went first because I had more points. He finished the round with 19 points, which was a very good score. His mom was there and she hugged and kissed him for doing so well. My mother was not in attendance, but I was the local kid from the neighborhood and everyone had picked me to win this competition. I managed to get 20 points and I won the championship. I was very happy, but this was not the only time I would compete against this young seven-year-old.

Dribble and Shoot

Two months after the Gino's Supper Shooter Contest, Mr. Durant asked me to enter another contest called Dribble and Shoot. In this contest, you still had to shoot from the free throw line and make layups, but you also had to dribble around four spaced out cones while being timed. This time I was first, and I ended with a twenty-point score in the shooting part and a thirty-second time in the dribbling. The young white kid, Mark, ended with nineteen points and a better time in the dribbling. He was declared the winner. I congratulated him on his win, but I was hurting because I had lost and many of the people from the recreation center were counting on me.

DISAPPOINTMENTS USUALLY FORM THE FOUNDATION OF OUR INITIAL DEVELOPMENTAL YEARS, BUT WE SHOULD NEVER ALLOW THEM TO DEFINE US.

Second Chance

After several weeks, the winner of the Dribble and Shoot would go on to compete at the Baltimore Civic Center in the next level of competition. But Mark was from out of town and could not Mr. attend, so Mr. Durant asked me to go in his place. I would get another chance to compete and I was determined to do better. I told him I needed to ask my mother first and raced home to tell her the good news. My mother smiled and said she would be there to watch, but she asked what I was competing for. I had not told her about competing in the dribble and shoot. I told her about the competition and she said, "I think you will do well."

I told Mr. Durant that my mother said I could compete, and he off ered to pick us up for the competition.

On the day of the competition, it was very cold outside. Mr. Durant picked us up on time, as planned. We made our way to the Baltimore Civic Center.

We entered through an entrance specifically used by those who were competing. In the locker room, there were all types of guys and girls of diff erent age groups and nationalities. Everyone was given instructions and I received a final pep talk from Mr. Durant. He said, "Ernie, you just go out there and you give it your best shot, just think about playing on the same basketball goals and court as the ones at Carroll Park."

I then walked down the tunnel to get to the basketball court. I looked out at the huge court. I kept thinking that this was the court where the Baltimore Bullets played and we were going to be allowed to stay and watch the game after competing. We walked over to the bench where the Bullets sat for their games. Five contestants were in my age bracket, and I was picked to go fifth.

The first contestant did well, with 18 points and a dribbling time of 25 seconds. The second contestant did well also, with 17 points and a dribbling time of 23 seconds. The third contestant, who was taller, and the most confident of all of us, said he was going to win this competition easily and that none of us could compete with him. He then proceeded to post a score and time of 19 points and 22 seconds. As he predicted, he was in first place. The fourth kid did well also, but not as good as the other contestants. He posted a score and time of 15 points and dribbling time of 35 seconds. He walked over to the sideline hurt and dejected, because he knew he could do better.

Finally, it was my turn. I looked into the crowd and became nervous to see all the people watching. I looked over at Mr. Durant and he was shouting, "Come on Ernie. You can do it." My mother was shouting also. In the shooting part of the competition, I posted a respectable 18 points. I proceeded to the dribbling part and I finished with a time of 26 seconds. The young, cocky kid finished in first place as he predicted. I finished in fourth place. I was very dejected because I knew I could have done better. We all received trophies for the place we finished. I congratulated all the participants.

 IT IS GOOD WHEN YOU CAN PUSH BEYOND YOUR OWN FAILURES AND DISSAPOINTMENTS TO CELEBRATE THE VICTORY OF OTHERS.

Family Background

As a kid, I was always good at sports, but life was not easy for me, my sisters, and brother. I am the youngest of four children. I have an older sister, Trevia. I have an older brother, who passed away in 1983; his name was Louis Molock. I have a younger sister, Shavon, nickname, Lady. My mother's name is Barbara Molock. We were a tight knit group growing up. Times were very hard for us. Our mother was on welfare for quite some time, but as luck would have it, one day the area school was hiring teacher aides and my mother landed a job. It was a good day for the Molock's.

I was really into sports. I received a scar on my face while trying to throw trash into a trash can, while in my underwear in the freezing icy rain. We didn't have much money, but my mother always ensured that we were fed and had clothes on our back. There were times when we did go without. We would go without electricity for days. We didn't have food for several days, and sometimes my mother would get food for us through credit at the corner store.

Where the Hell Is My Father

I used to walk around with holes in my shoes. I put cardboard in to cover the holes. It was a very embarrassing time, but my mother managed to keep us together and encouraged us to love one another and things would get better.

I used to have these shoes and the soles were coming off on both shoes. The neighborhood kids would make fun of my shoes, point them out to other people, and ask me to make my shoes clap. I would kick my feet in the air and my shoes would clap. As a kid, I could laugh with the other kids as they were teasing and making fun of me. But behind closed doors, it hurt very badly and I resented my mother for not being able to provide better for me. I often wondered, "Where the hell is my father." I knew my mother was doing the best she could for the four of us, but our situation was still hurtful.

I once tried out for a little league football team at the age of nine. I made the team and I was very proud of myself. I tried out for the team with my half-sole. Just think how much better I would have done if I had sneakers or cleats.

The Yankees

On the day I made the football team, I brought all my equipment home and I had to hide it from my mother. My mother did not want me to play football because my brother had gotten hurt and fractured his leg. I hid the equipment from my mother for two weeks. Then one day she said, "Ernie come in here I want to speak with you." I knew I was in trouble. She said, "Where did you get this equipment from?" I told her I made the football team. She told me I would not be playing. She made me turn in all the equipment and told me to find another sport to play. So I started playing baseball. I liked baseball, but not as much as I liked basketball.

At the end of March, registration for the Pig Town Little League Baseball began. I excitedly got a registration form and ran home to have my mother fill the form out, but there was the old familiar answer. My mother said she didn't have the money to pay the registration fee. I was once again hurt and dejected.

During this time, going to church played a big role in our lives. When I attended church that Sunday I asked God if there was a way I could play baseball. God answered my prayers, but it was not in the form of money for the registration fee. My friend Ray, who was a better baseball player then I was, asked if I would like to attend one of his baseball practices. I got all my gear and we started over to Carroll Park to practice. His team's name was the Dodgers.

When we took the field, I practiced hard and with passion because I wanted to show the coach and the rest of the players I was worthy of getting a spot on their team. After practice was over, the coach came over to me and put his hand on my shoulder and said, "Ernie you are a very good player, but I already have my roster of players." Once again, I was hurt. I thanked Ray for bringing me to practice with him and the coach for letting me practice. I headed home, with tears in my eyes when a voice called out to me, "Hey, let's talk for a minute." The voice belonged to Albert Cartright, a friend from school. We both attended the same classes. He told me his brother coaches the team he plays on called the Yankees. He asked if I could come out the next day, at the same time to practice with their team. I said, "Sure."

The next day I showed up and practiced hard and with passion. Albert's brother Oscar put his hand on my shoulder and said, "I thought you played very well in practice today. Did you fill out a registration form?" I told him I didn't have the money to pay the fee. He asked me if I would like to play for the Yankees. I told him yes and he welcomed me to the Yankees to play left field and pitching.

I ran all the way home to tell my mother the good news. She asked me how I made the team and said she had no money.

I told her I had practiced with the team and Oscar gave me a spot on the team and said he would pay the registration fee. I remember transitioning from crying to pure joy.

On the day of our first game, I was four for four with two home runs. I didn't pitch the first game, but I was scheduled to pitch the second game. The game was a showdown with the two projected best teams in the league, the Yankees and the Dodgers. The Dodgers were champions the year before and were picked to win the championship once again.

On that first day, my manager told me to do my best and we would win. The nervousness was running all through my body as I took the mound, but they were nerves of excitement. The game was a pitcher's duel for six straight innings. Then there was a break in the game. The Dodgers were the home team and we were the away team.

At the top of the seventh inning, our leadoff batter managed to get a walk to make it to first base. The next batter struck out. The next batter hit a ground ball to second base and our base runner made it to second base, but the batter was out at first. It was my turn at bat. With two outs in the top of the seventh inning, I had a chance to be a hero or a goat.

The Dodgers were undefeated and so were the Yankees. As I stepped up to the plate, I looked over to my coach. He was yelling. I knew what he was saying. It was my moment. I then looked down at third base where my friend Ray was. Our eyes met. He then went over to the pitcher's mound to give instructions to the pitcher. Ray and I played baseball in the neighborhood and many times we were both in this same situation. I knew he told the pitcher what he thought I would do in this situation, and I knew I would have to do something opposite. I was a straight fast ball hitter and I always pulled the ball to the left side of the field. After the first five pitches, it was a two and two count and all the pitches up to this point were inside. As I waited patiently, the pitcher made a mistake. He threw an outside pitch about waist high. I saw my chance and hit a line drive double into right field. My teammate scored from second base and we were winning one to nothing.

The next batter grounded out to first base, but we were excited about going into bottom of the seventh with a one to nothing lead. As I took the mound again, I was given instructions by the manager. I could only throw one pitch (a fastball). I didn't have a curve or a slider; it was a fastball every time, but I could throw faster than anyone in the league.

The first batter I would face was the second batter in the rotation for the Dodgers. I quickly threw three straight pitches to strike out the first batter. The next batter, Leon, would pose more of a problem. He was the opposing pitcher. Leon stepped up to the plate and he looked as cool as ever. My first pitch was a strike. The next pitch he lined deep into left field for a foul ball. I then threw a pitch low and away and he chased it to hit a ground ball to second base for the second out.

The next person to bat was my friend Ray. Once again we stared each other down and once again we were on familiar ground. My first pitch was a strike, which Ray swung at and missed. The next pitch was a fastball and he fouled it off to right field. Finally, this would be the pitch of the game. It was the bottom of the seven innings, with two outs, and all I needed was one more strike for my team to win the game. I knew my next pitch would have to be the best pitch I had ever thrown. I had already thrown two fastballs and Ray and

I both knew I was going to throw the same pitch again. I wound up and let go a fastball. Ray swung and missed, and we won the game. I was mobbed at the pitcher's mound. Ray and I looked at each other once again with respect.

We would go on to win many games. We would tie for first place with the Dodgers, because they would beat us the next time we played.

There was one more game that stood out as I remember my first season playing little league baseball—a game against the A's. The game was once again a one-run ball game. I was pitching once again and playing my heart out. My mother was on the sidelines watching for the first time. I wanted to make sure I showcased all my talents because she was watching.

The next person to bat was my friend Ray. Once again we stared each other down and once again we were on familiar ground. My first pitch was a strike, which Ray swung at and missed. The next pitch was a fastball and he fouled it off to right field. Finally, this would be the pitch of the game. It was the bottom of the seven innings, with two outs, and all I needed was one more strike for my team to win the game. I knew my next pitch would have to be the best pitch I had ever thrown. I had already thrown two fastballs and Ray and I both knew I was going to throw the same pitch again. I wound up and let go a fastball. Ray swung and missed, and we won the game. I was mobbed at the pitcher's mound. Ray and I looked at each other once again with respect.

We would go on to win many games. We would tie for first place with the Dodgers, because they would beat us the next time we played.

There was one more game that stood out as I remember my first season playing little league baseball—a game against the A's. The game was once again a one-run ball game. I was pitching once again and playing my heart out. My mother was on the sidelines watching for the first time. I wanted to make sure I showcased all my talents because she was watching.

WHAT CAUSES MANY OF US TO BE DERAILED FROM DOING GREATER THINGS, IS THAT WE TAKE SMALL OPPORTUNITIES WE ARE GIVEN FOR GRANTED.

At the end of a game, the coach would give a game ball to the player he thought played the best or helped the team win. There were no outs in the bottom of the seventh inning and we managed to get our leadoff hitter to second base with two outs. The next batter to the plate was Mattie, our shortstop. Mattie hit a double to right field and knocked in the winning run.

After the game, the coach sat us all on the bench and congratulated us. I just knew he was going to present me with the game ball, but he gave it to Mattie instead. I was very hurt because I thought for seven innings I was out there throwing that ball as hard as I could and I deserved to get the game ball. I went over to my mother and I was crying. She said she was happy our team won and she would take me to Gino's to get something to eat. My mother didn't have much money and when she said that, I stopped crying immediately and forgot all about the game. All I could think of was to get my hands on a Gino's giant. I will never forget that day. We went on to lose to the Dodgers in a five-game series 3-2.

In one of the games, we beat the Dodgers 2 to 1. I had a very good game. I knocked in one of the runs and caught three fly balls that would have been hits on another day, but this was the Championship. I thought I had a good all-around game and we would not have won without the plays I had made. At the end of the season, I did win most valuable player and received three trophies at the end-of-year banquet. We also earned the respect of the Dodger players and coaches, so much that we were asked to hoist the Championship trophy together.

My First Job

After that season, I continued playing little league baseball until I was sixteen years old. During this time, a friend of the family recommended me for a job with Thomas Scherr's Groceries, the neighborhood store. Mr. Tommy was a Caucasian store owner who was a fixture in the Pig Town neighborhood. He would often give credit to families who were not able to pay for their groceries until the beginning of the month when the welfare check came out. I earned six dollars a day after school for three hours of work, Monday through Friday. I earned twelve dollars on Saturdays for 8 hours of work and six dollars on Sundays. I have so many memories of working for Mr. Tommy, but I will stick to the thing I most vividly remember.

As a young kid, I observed how Mr. Tommy conducted business. He kept a ledger that contained information about everyone in the neighborhood who owed him money. I found my mother's name in the ledger and at that moment I knew I was going to do something about my mother's situation. I didn't know how but I knew something had to be done. Mr. Tommy had a lunch meat cutting machine and I was responsible for cleaning it every night. One night I was cleaning the machine while the blade was turning. The blade caught some of my fingers and I almost went into shock. I was bleeding badly and almost blacking out. Mr. Tommy managed to stop the bleeding and we joked about it later.

One time when all my work was done, Mr. Tommy and I were just having a casual conversation. He reminded me that one day while playing with my friends and running past his store, I yelled, "Hey, Mr. Tommy, you big-nose bitch." I pretended I did not remember, but I did. We must always be careful how we treat others, as it could seriously impact our own future. It was a good thing Mr. Tommy didn't hold a grudge.

 BE CAREFUL HOW YOU TREAT OTHERS, REGARDLESS OF THEIR RACE, CLASS, OR RELIGIOUS PERSUASION.

Taking on Responsibility

My mother sat me down one day and told me that I had to give up half my salary. I didn't understand her request, and I cried for two days. My mother explained to me that everyone in the house was expected to put money in the pot for the good of the family. She said I would not understand now, but I would once I got older and that this builds character. Both my sisters were not working and my brother had his own paper route. I wondered if he was putting any money in the pot. I felt it was my money, so why did I have to share half with the family? They didn't earn this money. Deep down inside I knew it was because my mother needed help feeding and clothing us.

My home life wasn't the greatest and there were many embarrassing moments. There were times when we did not have any food in the refrigerator, and I mean none. The only thing we had were ice cubes. There were times when our electricity was turned off for days at a time and we had to wait until my mother got her check at the beginning of the month to get the lights turned on. We had to light candles at night and we read comic books because we could not watch TV. Our friends would come by and yell in our window or through the door, "Hey, Ernie, is your gas and electricity off again? What happened? Your mother didn't pay the light bill again." I was so embarrassed and hurt. I promised myself that when I became a man, I would never go without food, gas, and electricity. Because of my childhood experiences, I was determined to make something out of my life and work my tail off to get the things my mother could not get for me.

I was no different from any other child. I wasn't a bad child who did illegal things. I was a busybody. I would get into everything. I had gotten into trouble for things I had done. I don't remember all of them.

When I was thirteen, a friend of the family caught me trying to have sex with one of the neighborhood girls in the back of his car. Mr. Pete's car door was unlocked and I talked the young lady into getting into the car with me. I then put newspaper up around all the windows. I managed to kiss her a few times and then started taking off her clothes. She began to help me get her clothes off and then I started taking off my clothes while she was taking hers off. I was about to lay on top of her when the car door opened and it was Mr. Pete. I was standing in the car with my pants down by my ankles and all my business showing. He grabbed me by the forearm and led me to my mother with my pants around my ankles. He did not allow me to pull up my underwear.

My mother was shocked and asked what was going on. Mr. Pete said, "I found your son in my car trying to have sex with a young lady." My mother's jaw dropped and she immediately took me home and gave me one of the worst spankings I ever got.

On another occasion, I was playing on the railroad tracks near where I lived and a policeman showed up (we called them the railroad dicks). I threw a couple of rocks at him and told him to kiss my ass. It was a very nice, bright, and sunny day and I started running. The police officer gave chase. I tried all kinds of tricks to get away from him, but I couldn't. I ran through alleys, I took short cuts but I could not get him off my tail.

Finally, I started running towards home and I ran up the street I lived on. I was a few steps ahead of the police officer as I was running up the street. The people on the block were calling out to me. Two seconds behind me was a police officer chasing me. It was a sight to see.

I finally got to my house and ran past my mother. Before she could ask what was happening, there was a knock at the door. By this time, I was over in the corner crying my eyes out because I knew I was about to get into some serious trouble.

The police officer told my mother everything, and then he left. My mother turned to me with blood in her eyes and gave me the worst punishment ever. I could not go outside for three whole days. It was summertime and for three days, I was miserable. When my friends passed by, my mother told them I couldn't go out to play.

 PARENTAL DISCIPLINE PLAYS A SIGNIFICANT AND MAJOR ROLE IN A CHILD'S DEVELOPMENT. THEY ARE LESSONS A CHILD NEVER FORGETS.

Sibling Rivalry

There was another time in my young age when there were sibling situations. My older sister, Trebie, and my older brother, Louis, were always doing things that involved my younger sister, Lady, and me. Lady and I knew these things were wrong, but they would threaten to beat us up if we said anything to mother. Trebie would often let boys into the house when our mother wasn't there. They weren't doing anything. She just liked the company.

My brother was the one that would get all of us in trouble most of the time. One day Louis stayed outside way pass his curfew. When he came home, it was 1 AM. He knocked on the back window where he and I shared a bedroom. I went downstairs to open the door and as soon as I opened it, my mother was standing right behind me. She made both of us strip down to our underwear and stand outside next to our house. It was 30 degrees outside. I looked over at my brother and he looked at me. He knew my thoughts. I was never going to do this again.

Chapter 2

MY JUNIOR YEARS

"Life is a struggle. Life will throw curveballs at you, it will humble you, it will attempt to break you down. And just when you think things are starting to look up, life will smack you back down with ruthless indifference."

As I grew older, I became better at playing basketball and I also began to get taller and stronger. I would practice in the rain and I would shovel the snow off the court to be able to practice.

My brother had always been better at baseball and basketball, and I had never beaten him. He was bigger, stronger, faster, and more skilled. One day he asked to play me in a one-on-one basketball game. I beat him that day by one point. After I beat him I was so excited. I started to jeer him. This did not sit well with my brother and he chased me around the court for twenty minutes. I was screaming for Ma. My brother never played basketball with me again.

As I got a little older, I got a job with the summer youth work program, so I informed Mr. Tommy I would be leaving. He did not want me to leave and he would say little negative things to get me to continue to work with him. I told Mr. Tommy this was an opportunity for me to make more money, to help my mother out more, and to purchase better clothes and shoes for myself. Mr. Tommy was a good man and he understood in the end. He only asked that I find a nice young kid in the neighborhood as a replacement. I already had a replacement in mind. The kid's name was Stevie Whitney, and both Mr. Tommy and I agreed. This was the end of my career as a stock boy with the corner store.

 LIFE IS FILLED WITH TRANSITIONAL MOMENTS, AND WE MUST KNOW WHEN IT IS TIME TO MOVE ON.

As I moved on to my summer job, I was excited about the opportunity to make more money. The job would start at the end of the school year, and I would work full-time hours as a janitorial assistant for the whole summer. The job would also continue into the fall and spring as an afternoon job. The job consisted of cleaning floors, wiping walls, cleaning the grounds, etc. There were six of us and we would be working at Charles Barrister Carroll Elementary School under the supervision of Mrs. Anita Curry. What was special about this location was that all of us: Ray, Phillip, Michael, David, Thomas, and myself were all graduates of this elementary school. Also, Michael's mother and my mother worked there as teacher's aides.

The first summer of working at the school was great. Mrs. Curry would often invite us over to her house after work or on the weekend and she would feed us. Mrs. Curry sure could cook.

When I got my first check, the first thing I bought was a pair of shell head Adidas basketball shoes—they were white with black stripes. I thought my shoes were the best thing ever. I could also give my mother some money and it felt very good to do that. I could give her money and it did not feel as though I didn't have any left, like it felt when I gave her half the money I made as a stock boy.

After my first summer job, I was due to start the 10th grade in the fall. I was excited and scared at the same time. I remember going to Southwestern Senior High and thinking the school was so big and intimidating. I should not have felt this way because my two cousins, Wayne and Hope, attended the school and my sister Lady attended also. Lady sat me down and she talked with me for about an hour.

My first year went by pretty fast and there are many things I could point out, but there are always some things that stick out more than others. I was able to make friends very quickly. Homeroom was the class where everyone would meet in the morning before separating to go to other classes. I learned very quickly if someone told a joke about you, then you had to fire back immediately with a joke about them. There were always jokes about one's clothing or their mama or how they looked. I became so good at my comebacks that no one would say too many things bad about me. I once told a friend his mother WAS so stupid, she thought menopause was a button on a VCR.

The one major thing that stands out about my freshman year in high school is this. Lady had a friend named Bernita who was about six feet, two inches tall and in high school. She was a giant compared to most girls her age. She weighed about two hundred pounds and it was not fat. She carried it well. No one messed with Bernita. I was afraid of her also. But she was a friend of my sister, who thought Bernita was the nicest person in the world.

One day in the cafeteria, one of my friends sat in the seat where Bernita always sat and everyone was telling him to move. He didn't, claiming he was not afraid of her. Bernita showed up, marched over to her favorite seat, and told my friend to move. She was very calm and she did not pressure him in anyway. He said, "I am not afraid of you Bernita. You may have everyone else around here afraid of you, but I am not. I am going to sit wherever the hell I please." Bernita grabbed him by his collar and dragged him across the table where we were sitting. She threw him to the floor. When she was dragging him across the table, we all picked up our trays and watch him go pass. Bernita then made a small conversation with me, and went to sit in her favorite seat. From that day on, Bernita and I were friends and no one would bother me or talk against me. By the end of my first year, I had more friends than my sister.

 A WISE MAN ONCE WROTE, THE ONE WHO WANTS TO HAVE FRIENDS, MUST FIRST SHOW HIMSELF TO BE FRIENDLY.

Making the Team

In the morning, before class, they allowed us to play basketball in the gym for about a half an hour. I got there extra early to try and get picked to play because I wanted to show the guys what I could do. It was hard to get a chance to play, because the seniors dominated the court.

One day I managed to get a chance to play because my cousin, Wayne, was a senior and he suggested me to one of his friends. I did very well. The games were only to six points because of the time. I managed to make three baskets and the seniors were happy for me and they congratulated me. After that, I was picked every morning to play.

Several of the seniors asked why I didn't go out for the JV basketball team. At this time, I would have to make a decision that would be a recurring decision for the next twenty years. I had many responsibilities to think of before I could make that decision. I liked the fact that I was working at Charles Carroll Barrister, and I could buy nice clothes, so my friends wouldn't pick on me anymore. I was helping my mother out with bills and I would give Lady money from time to time. It felt good to be responsible and needed, but deep inside I would love to have been playing basketball for the high school. As I entered my junior year in high school, my friends asked if I was going to play basketball that year. I said no because I had too much responsibility and because I liked having money of my own. I didn't have anyone encouraging me to go for my dream of becoming an NBA player and I had reservations myself. People kept telling me to go after my dream. There were many things going on in my life.

YOUR DREAM WILL ALWAYS BE THAT
REALITY THAT LOOKS LIKE IT WILL COST
YOU EVERYTHING TO GO AFTER IT.

I remember an incident that happened while I was attending Harlem Park Junior High School that would prove noteworthy in my junior year of high school. When I was in junior high, one day I decided to leave school early, which was something I would never do because there was no one at home during the day. I was walking from school and came upon five boys my age. One of the boys asked me for money. I knew these guys were going to beat me up, so I punched the guy who was talking in the face as hard as I could and I started running. They all started chasing me. I was running as fast as I could. I came upon a railroad bridge that separated our section of the city from the section where the guys chasing me were from.

Some Caucasian guys I went to school with started throwing rocks at the guys chasing me. This allowed me to get under the bridge and once under the bridge, I waved at the guys and said thanks.

During my junior year in high school, race relations were pretty bad, but I got along with all my friends; black and white. During this time, the African American series "Roots" aired on television. This would prove to be a significant time in my life because of the hatred one person can show towards another.

Whenever a white person showed up at school, they were being beaten up by several black students just because they were white and because of the things happening in "Roots." I remember walking down the hill from our school after class was over and I was walking with a friend—the same guy who spoke to me and threw rocks at the guys who were chasing me when I was in junior high school. Several guys surrounded us and they wanted to beat him up. I stood to defend him. I was a bit well known at the school. The guys ran down the hill and my friend thanked me. We went down the hill together to catch the bus because we were from the same neighborhood. Again, this is a powerful lesson on doing to others what you would have them do to you.

 LIFE IS A CYCLE AND MANY TIMES THE KINDNESS YOU SHOW TO OTHERS, IS RETURNED TO YOU, AND SOMETIMES IN AN EVEN GREATER MEASURE.

I was becoming increasingly well known around the high school and people continuously asked if I was going to play basketball next year for the school. I just could not see how I could fit basketball into my schedule. I didn't want to give up my afterschool job, but I really did want to play.

As luck would have it, or maybe fate, the principal at the school where I worked hired another worker during the summer after my junior year. This proved to be significant.

Mr. Campbell hired Ray Hale—my old friend who played baseball for the little league Dodgers team when I played for the Yankees. When Ray was hired, he was able to continue to play baseball at Poly High School and still keep his job. He still received a check even though he was not at work. I decided to take this situation to our supervisor Mrs. Anita Curry. When I explained the situation to Mrs. Curry, she said I have nothing to do with that because he was hired by Mr.

Campbell and he was a favorite of Mr. Campbell. I told her it would be very unfair if I was given the same treatment. I wanted to speak with Mr. Campbell, but Mrs. Curry advised me to leave it alone. I could not, so I decided to meet with Mr. Campbell. Our meeting went better than I expected. I was under the impression that he was going to deny my request, but he was very supportive. He told me I could play high school sports, but to remember my education comes first and playing sports is just a part of that education. I left his office very excited. That year was 1980 and the summer came and went so quickly.

In the fall, I had my sights set on trying out for the Southwestern High School basketball team, and I let everyone know. During the next few weeks I would hear different stories about the coach and what he liked in a player.

On the day of tryouts, Coach Swartz walked in the gym and said we were going to all work hard and everyone would get an opportunity to prove himself worthy to make the team. I don't know what everyone else heard, but once I heard "opportunity," that meant I had a chance to make the starting line-up. I knew some of the players already, because I had been playing against them in the morning before school started. One of the players was also my cousin, Guy Bell.

We practiced for several days and on the final day cuts would be made. Coach Swartz had to cut the roster to twelve players. The final practice ended on a Thursday and Coach said the list would be posted in the morning to see who made the team. I was very nervous about checking the list.

Some guys checked the list as soon as the bell sounded in the morning the next day. I waited. I could pick out those who did not make it because they came to class dejected. I did not ask if anyone had seen my name on the list.

After a few class periods, I got up the nerve to go check the list. I didn't make it. My cousin Guy found me in the hall and said he would get me on the team. I was so excited but I kept my cool because I didn't want anyone to see how excited I was. I went down to the gym just to read my name on the list. We would go on to have a 500 season and along the way we would compete against many future NBA players. Our team competed against the likes of David Wingate, Reggie Williams, Tyrone (Mugsy) Bogues of Dunbar High School, and Spoon James of Walbrook High to name a few.

 WE NEVER TRULY KNOW WHO WE ARE CROSSING PATHS WITH IN THE PRESENT, BUT OFTEN TIMES OUR PRESENT INTERACTIONS WILL GIVE US A GLIMPSE OF THE FUTURE.

During practices, the coach would pit the red team against the blue team. The red team consisted of all the seniors and players from the previous year. The blue team consisted of sophomores and new comers to the team. In the first game, the red team beat the blue team easily, but after that beating, the blue team would not lose to the red team again during that season. I was part of the blue team and the coach noticed that I was the one leading them. This eff ort helped me crack the starting lineup.

The first game I played in the starting lineup was against Poly High School. Poly played a very good game and the score was close throughout the entire game. I was excited to play against Poly because I had two friends who attended Poly: Carl Waters and Ray Hale, the same Ray Hale I worked with at my afterschool job. I grew up with both these guys.

Carl was a very good player and I knew he could have made the Poly team. The game went back and forth throughout and with thirty seconds left, I was fouled driving to the basket. I was hit in the mouth and I was woozy and bleeding. I got to the free throw line and I was nervous, because we were playing on their home court and all the people were screaming for me to miss the free throws. I managed to make both free throws and we then stole the ball on the inbounds pass to win the game by two points. I finished the game with thirteen points, eight rebounds and six assists. I didn't care what my statistics were. I was just glad we won. We would go on to finish the season with a 500 record and, considering how we started, this was a great accomplishment.

At the school banquet, I received a trophy for the most improved player. After the banquet Coach Swartz called four of us into his office to discuss our future. Coach presented one of three scholarships to Keith Smith, who was a returning player who played baseball, football, and basketball. The coach called his name for a full scholarship to one of the area colleges. Austin Coates was the best player on our team and the leading scorer; he also received a full scholarship. The third scholarship would go to another person whose name I cannot remember. All three were very happy and I was very happy for them. Coach then sat me down and explained that he wished he had a fourth scholarship. He was really upset he didn't have another scholarship, and I didn't understand why because I didn't know what was going on as a teenager. I was just happy for the guys. It wasn't until after I graduated high school that I understood why coach was upset. Once you graduate high school, you better have a plan for the future, because life comes at you pretty fast when you have no clue what your next move is going to be. Coach was upset because he knew that with a scholarship I would have something to look forward to and an opportunity to improve my life. I was very disappointed, but at that age I didn't really understand the magnitude of what it all meant.

 WE DON'T ALWAYS GET WHAT WE WANT IN LIFE, EVEN WHEN WE DESERVE TO, AND EVERYONE AROUND US IS CONVINCED THAT WE SHOULD. SOMETIMES, LIFE JUST HAS SOMETHING ELSE IN MIND.

After the basketball season ended, all my classmates began to talk of the senior prom and graduation. I was friends with many young ladies while in high school, but I didn't have a girlfriend. I was interested in Donna, a young lady from the neighborhood. My second choice was Wanda. One day while in homeroom class, we were all taking about who to ask to the prom. Donna explained she would be taking a college gentleman to the prom. I was surprised by her answer, because I had intended to ask her since we were both from the same neighborhood. I then turned my focus to Wanda, but as outgoing as I am, I could not bring myself to ask her. I just couldn't get up the nerve. After a few weeks, I finally asked her, and she said she already had a date. I was crushed. The prom was soon approaching and I needed to find a date.

NEVER DECIDE TO DELAY GRABBING AN OPPORTUNITY BECAUSE OF FEAR AND UNCERTAINTY. YOU WILL REGRET IT.

Proms are usually very nice and, during the senior year, many students drive to their prom. I didn't have a license or a car and I was in dire straits about who I was going to take and how I was going to get to the prom.

I finally got the nerve to ask another young lady from the neighborhood whom I was good friends with and she had a car. She was my cousin's girlfriend and we all thought it would be a good idea. I was so excited to finally have a date. Her name was Sugar and she was beautiful.

The Prom finally came around and all my friends were there. Sugar also recognized many people because they were from the same neighborhood. Sugar and I danced a few times, but I knew I could only get so close because Sugar was my cousin's girlfriend. I told Sugar I was going to mingle a little with my friends and she should do the same. I spotted Wanda and I walked over to see how she was doing. Wanda had lied to me. She did not have a date and I was grinning from ear to ear. I asked her if she would like to dance. She asked about my date. I explained that Sugar and I were just friends from the neighborhood. I spent most of the rest of the prom dancing with Wanda.

I that I had not seen Donna and wondered why she was not at the prom. Sugar and I danced a few more times and afterward she dropped me off and then went home. That was the end of a good night.

The Monday following prom night, all of us in homeroom were talking about our prom experience and everyone said they had a good time. I asked Donna why we did not see her at the prom. She said she did not come because I did not ask her. We all looked at each other. I reminded her that she said she was bringing a college student. She wanted me to ask anyway. I was no mind reader, so we both missed that opportunity.

 WOMEN ARE A MYSTERY. THEY WILL DO CRAZY THINGS JUST TO TEST HOW MUCH YOU REALLY WANT WHAT YOU ARE ASKING FOR.

The Graduation

The next thing on the docket was the graduation itself. Everyone was excited about graduating from high school. Some students had plans, but many did not know what they were going to do with the rest of their lives. I was one of those who didn't know what I was going to do.

 LESSON FOR PARENTS AND TEACHERS; DON'T LET OUR KIDS LEAVE HIGH SCHOOL WITHOUT A PLAN.

I decided I would look for a permanent job with full-time hours once I got out of school and my job with Barrister Charles Carroll was over. I worked at Barrister Charles Carroll until I could no longer work there. My supervisor

Mrs. Curry would give me as many hours as she could, but she informed me that she would have to let me go. Once again, I pondered the idea of what I was going to do once I stopped working for the school. I would have the whole summer to think about it.

 TO LIVE UNDER THE SHADOW OF OUR PARENTS IS GOOD FOR A SEASON, BUT WE MUST ALWAYS BE CONSCIOUS THAT A TIME WILL COME, AND IT WILL COME FAST AND HARD, WHEN WE HAVE TO STAND ON OUR OWN TWO FEET.

Chapter 3

ENTERING COLLEGE

"Most of the important things in the world have been accomplished by people who have kept on trying when there seemed to be no hope at all."

~ DALE CARNEGIE

My brother Louis put the idea of college in my head, but I did not want to go. I though all I needed was a job, so I could continue making money. I did not know I was not making that much money, but it seemed to be enough at the time. Louis said I needed to invest in my future for better opportunities. After giving the idea much thought, I decided to attend the same college my brother was attending, Coppin State College. This decision made my mother very happy and proud. She would have two children in college. When she talked about it, she lit up like a Christmas tree.

THE POWER OF COMMUNITY IS THAT PEOPLE AROUND US WILL ALWAYS SEE WHAT WE CAN'T SEE. ALL ADVICE THAT COMES FROM OTHERS SHOULD BE GIVEN DUE DILIGENCE. IT CAN HELP US DECIDE ON THE NEXT STEP WE ARE SUPPOSED TO TAKE.

I submitted all paper work and was due to attend Coppin State College in the fall of 1982. When I walked onto the College campus, the place was huge. My brother told me to just go to class, keep my grades up, and I would be fine. I was scared at first, but I took comfort in knowing he was on the campus somewhere. He would leave the campus to go to work at 1 PM.

I took many prerequisites during my first semester. I had a full eighteen credits. Most of my courses consisted of English, Math, and History. As the months moved along, I made friends and did well in my classes. I became comfortable with the campus and I only saw my brother sparingly.

Halfway through the semester, I decide to apply for work study to earn a paycheck. This decision would prove be a very good one. I applied at the Parlett Moore Library and Robinette Smith hired me immediately. I was so excited to be hired for a job. I was excited to be able to help my mother out again. I was excited to be working in the library, because I could also research information and I had a place to get my homework done before and after classes.

While working at the library, I met and became friends with people who would become significant in my life. Robinette was a very good supervisor and she taught me many things.

I learned from her experience for three years and enjoyed it. What was great about work study was you could work full-time during the summer. It helped me to save money and buy the different things I would need for the upcoming semesters.

Meeting My Best Friends

In the spring of 1983, I met Gwen Oliver, who would become my best friend on the campus. Gwen also worked in the library, for the director, Mr. Boyce. When we met, we immediately liked each other. I thought Gwen was very beautiful and very intelligent. As our friendship grew, we often went to lunch together or just talked about college or our future. I often went to her house to spend the evening and occasionally she came to my house.

I also met

After I finished working for Robinette, the library was going to let me go. But Mrs. Dorothy Rather interceded so I could continue to work for her at the library. Mrs. Rather would prove to be a nurturing and caring mother figure in my life who would help me stay grounded. We became very close. I could tell Mrs. Rather anything and she would not judge me. She would be very stern with me and she told it like it was. If I was wrong, she would tell me. If I did something she approved of, she would also tell me.

Kathleen Patterson was and still is a very good friend. I could go to Kathy because she understood some of the stresses of college. She would often help me determine how to complete an assignment.

The year 1983 proved to be a very good year and the most challenging year of my life. On the Coppin campus, there were eight women to every one man on campus. I met many, many women.

Karen Spruill also worked with Mrs. Rather, and we became very good friends. Pixie was an athlete like me. She was very nice and had a great personality. We became very good friends also.

Tragedy

During the spring semester of 1983 I would endure happiness and sorrow. I met a young lady and knew immediately she was a woman I could marry. It just wasn't a good time. I was in college and too young to be thinking of marriage. I thought this was my time to explore and to concentrate on my studies.

While we were on break before the beginning of Spring semester 1983. I was lying in bed one day and I received a phone call from the state police. The young lady asked to speak to my mother and I said my mother was at work. She then asked if I knew Louis Molock. My heart was racing. I told her he was my brother. She then said he'd been in a very bad accident. Louis was hit by an eighteen-wheeler truck and was being transported to the shock trauma unit at the University of Maryland Hospital. I was shocked and knew I had to tell my mother immediately. I dropped the phone and ran to her job at Barrister Charles Carroll Elementary, which was just around the corner.

When I arrived, I was crying and I asked if I could speak with Barbara Molock. It was an emergency. When my mother came to the front office, she could see on my face that something was terribly wrong and she said, "Ernie what is wrong; calm down and tell me what is wrong." I said, "Ma, Louis has been in a very bad accident and they are transporting him to University of Maryland shock trauma unit." My mother started crying. We both left the school to go to the hospital.

Once we had told my two sisters, we all went to the hospital to find out the prognosis. My mother could not contain herself. She feared the worst.

At the hospital, the doctor explained that Louis was in a coma and that if he regained consciousness, he would be no more than a grapefruit. He also explained that the machine was helping to keep Louis alive. They would give it a few days to see what happened, but it didn't look good.

We all took turns going to see Louis, and some days it appeared he was getting better and knew someone was in the room with him. After two weeks had passed, the doctor met with my mother and the rest of the family. No family should ever have to face what we went through in that moment. The doctor explained that Louis had not been responding to treatment and our insurance did not cover the cost to keep him on the machine. My mother was faced with a decision that would haunt her for the rest of her life. She would have to decide to pull the plug or the doctors were going to do it anyway. My mother decided to have the plug pulled. I don't remember the date, but my brother died in February 1983.

IF YOU LIVE LONG ENOUGH, AT SOME POINT YOU WILL HAVE TO PAUSE LIFE TO DEAL WITH GRIEF AND TRAUMA. IT IS AN OVERWHELMING SEASON IN LIFE THAT ONLY TIME CAN HEAL.

Louis had many friends at Coppin State College, and he was due to graduate in the spring of 1983. A memorial service was held for Louis at the Jacobs Building on the College campus. Many of his friends and professors attended. It would take some doing to get over the passing of my brother but I had to move on. I didn't know if I wanted to stay in college afterward. He was the person who talked me into going in the first place.

In May of 1983, during commencement, I was asked to sit in the seat that would have been my brother's and accept his degree. As I sat down, a young lady said, "Where have you been? You are late getting here." Another young woman said, "He is the brother of the guy who was in the bad car accident." The other young lady then apologized.

When Louis's name was called, there was an applause for him and his achievements. Louis was very smart—much smarter than me. He was the type of person who could look at information once and could recall the same information word for word. I had to work very hard to get the grades I received, and they were mostly lower B's and C's.

Once Louis's name was called, and I got up to walk across the stage, I knew in that instance that I had to finish college not only for myself, but for Louis because that is what he would want me to do. I felt so proud to walk across the stage and receive my brother's degree.

Moving On

As I grew more comfortable with the death of my brother, I began to make new friends and meet more people. I became very fond of one of my teachers, Mrs. JoAnn Martin. Mrs. Martin ran the English skills lab where all students could get help if they were falling behind in English. Mrs. Martin knew my brother, and she often told stories about him. She also helped keep me in line because all my professors knew I had a good relationship with Mrs. Martin on a personal and professional level. I respected her opinion of my progression as a college student.

One day while in English class, I received a note from two young ladies in the back of the class, asking why I wore a hood to cover my face when I walked across the campus every day. One was asking for a date. I thought it was a bit forward, but I was flattered. The young lady's name was Renae Sparks. I didn't know it at the time, but she would soon play a very significant role in my life.

Once Renae and I became involved, it spread throughout the campus. Many of my friends, for example, Gwen, Karen, Kathy, Pixie, Mrs. Rather, and others, asked if Renae was my girlfriend. I didn't answer them directly. All of them gave me flack about my relationship with Renae.

More and more, Renae and I were together on campus. My male friends started asking, "Hey Moe, is this your girlfriend?" One day, someone asked the question while we were walking on campus together, and it became clear that I could not dance around the question. Renae and I looked at each other, and I said, "Yes she is." From that moment on, people asked about us wherever I went. And whenever

Renae walked by, people would say to me, "There goes your girlfriend" or "Here comes your girlfriend." Renae was my girlfriend; it was a situation I could handle and I liked it.

Renae and I began to spend more and more time together. I knew she was the woman I could marry, but this was my college year and I was not quite ready for that type of commitment. We went to movies and to lunch together and got along fine, until it happened.

The Breakup

One day Renae said she could no longer be my girlfriend because she consistently heard many stories about me and other girls. I did not deny that I knew many other girls, but they were not my girlfriends.

I had given her money to hold for me so we could go shopping. She gave me the money back and walked off.

After the break up, I often watched her walk across the campus from the library. When we passed each other, we said hello, but she would not hold a conversation with me. I saw her talking with other guys and it was apparent to me that she had moved on.

Renae then joined the sorority organization "the Persian Angels." During this time, she would ask me to get her food and to watch over her while she got a nap between classes, while she was pledging. I was not the kind of person who wanted to join a fraternity, but I was approached by all the fraternities on campus.

Renae attended Coppin for three semesters and then she left to concentrate on her full-time job. We remained friends, but eventually we fell out of touch with each other and she only called me once a month or once every two months.

I moved on, but I always thought of Renae from time to time.

 HEARTBREAK IS A PART OF LIFE'S JOURNEY. IT PREPARES US SOMEHOW FOR LIFELONG COMMITMENTS.

Getting Back in the Game

I moved into my junior year and decided to try out for the basketball team. I was already playing against some of the players on the team and I thought I would have a good chance of making the team as a walk-on.

On the day of tryouts, I was surprised to see so many guys there to try out for the team. After the first week, the coach, whose name was Bates, cut the roster to twenty players. He then cut the roster to twelve players. I was nervous, but I still thought I had a good shot.

At the end of two weeks, Coach Bates said he would post the final roster on the door outside his office at 9am Monday morning. We all had the weekend to think about our possibilities of making the team. The exceptions were the scholarship players, who knew they were on the team.

Monday morning came and I was in familiar territory. I didn't want to rush over to see the roster for fear of not making the team. Once again, a friend, who also tried out for the team, spoiled it for me. "Moe, guess what? You made the team," he said. I stopped for a minute. I was going to be on a college basketball team. I was very happy.

When I went to the library for work that day I told everyone I had made the basketball team. Everyone was happy for me, especially Mrs. Rather and Mrs. Smith. Practice would be that Monday at 3 PM. We were a .500 basketball team and always gave our best eff ort. We were an undersized team and most teams we played against were a lot bigger than us. We never got blown out of games, but we just didn't have the size to compete late in games. I don't remember all the games, but some do stand out more than others. I didn't play much as a walk on, but every now and then I would get into a game.

Our division was the Mid-Eastern Atlantic Conference (MEAC). I do remember four games. We played against the University of Bridgeport. I remember this game because it was billed for us to play against the tallest player in the conference. As we were warming up for the game, we were all excited to see who this tall player was that everyone was making such a fuss about.

Then it happened. The announcer called out from East Sudan, Africa, Manute Bol. Yes! It was Manute Bol. When he came into the arena, he had to bend so far down just to get through the door. All of us were amazed at how tall he was. We lost that game. He blocked every shot from our team that came into the painted area.

After this game, I nearly quit the team. I explained to him that my grades were beginning to slip and I needed to leave the team to concentrate more on my studies. The coach advised me to take some less challenging classes. He would talk with some of the instructors. I told him I would buckle down and accept any grade that I was due.

After my talk with coach, I started managing my time better and I pulled my grades up before the end of the semester.

The next game I remember is the game against Hampton University. This time we were able to win the game with four minutes left when the coach put me in the game. I managed to secure a triple double, two points, two assists, and two rebounds.

Before I got into the game, and while I was sitting on the bench, one of my teammates tapped me on the shoulder and said, "Moe, there is a young lady five rows back who would like to speak with you." I thought they were playing a trick on me. After the game when I emerged from the locker room, there was this beautiful young lady standing in the hallway. She said hi. All my teammates were standing off to the side wondering why this beautiful woman wanted to talk with me. I was wondering the same thing. Her name was Jeanie.

I asked her about her interest. I ride the bench and I am not one of the star players, and I don't play very much. She said, "I know all that and the reason I wanted to talk with you is because I think you are handsome and it is never the star player who makes a good boyfriend or husband. It is most often the guy who rides the bench. And I can see in you that you are a good person. I would like to give you my number and when I come to Baltimore, I would like to get together and have dinner." Before I could stop grinning from ear to ear, I gave Jeanie my number. We hugged and she said I will see you in Baltimore. She did come to Baltimore, but she did not catch up with me. I only know she came because she left a message on my answering machine.

The Last Game of The Season

The last game I remember was a game against Florida A&M University (FAMU). It was the last game of the season and Coach Bates told everyone we were flying to Florida. I had never been on a plane and I was excited. We also received tickets to go to Disney World, and we would be in Florida for three days. We would stay at a nice hotel. It just seemed like the perfect sports trip.

We had such a wonderful time with all the festivities. We met some young ladies from Michigan. We went to Disney World, and we saw some historical places. On the day of the game, FAMU beat us easily. We were all tired from the festivities and from staying up late. The coach told all of us to go to sleep early. We finished the season as a 500. We were pleased with our record. We were not the same team we were at the beginning of the season. We developed into a more respectable team than our record indicated.

Basketball League

The season ended and it was time to enjoy time off . As the summer began, I got this idea to have a summer basketball league in the neighborhood where I grew up. I pitched the idea to Arthur White, the perfect guy to be the commissioner and help me get the league started. He immediately said it was a great idea and we began to take steps to initiate our own neighborhood basketball league. We called it the Pigtown Neighborhood Basketball League. The League consisted of five teams: the 76ers, the Celtics, the Nets, the Lakers, and the Bombers. All the teams consisted of players from the neighborhood and were evenly matched.

SOME OF THE GREATEST SPORTS STARS PARTICIPATED IN OR INITIATED COMMUNITY SPORTS IN THEIR NEIGHBORHOOD.

When I put together the rosters, I paired all the teams with young and older players, with good players and some not so good players. Everyone was happy with their team and the neighborhood buzzed with anticipation for the league to begin. During the season, the whole neighborhood turned out to watch the fun-filled games.

After the games, many of the players drank beer with the team. They just played and talked of key plays in the game and it was all good fun. I was the leader and coach of my team, the 76ers. We were known as the young team because the rest of my team was younger than me. We went on to post league's best record and we would go into the playoff s as the number one team.

There would be one playoff game among the other four teams and the winner of that series of playoff games would play the 76ers; a best of three series to determine the Champion. We were pretty sure we would play against the Celtics.

During the regular season, we split with the Celtics and every game was close. The Celtics were the team I feared the most because they were loaded with experienced players and they were a little older than my team and a bit more seasoned. The Celtics took the first game of the series and this crushed my young players because they didn't know how to handle this defeat. I gathered all of them together and we practiced before the next game. I explained to them that it was only one game and if we stayed focus and played hard and aggressive, we could still win the series. We went on to win the second game and tie the series. We were the favorite team in the neighborhood and every team wanted to beat the 76ers. The other teams that were now out of the playoff s wanted the Celtics to beat our team.

 A SIGNIFICANT CHARACTERISTIC OF ANY GREAT LEADER IS THEIR NATURAL ABILITY TO MOTIVATE THEIR TEAM MEMBERS TO GO ABOVE AND BEYOND.

In the decisive third game, the Celtics were ahead with a large lead. This lead crushed my young team and they all looked to me for what to do. We started to come back midway through the first half. As the leader of my team, I was determined we were not going down without a fight. The Celtics were up by 18 points. I hit five straight shots to cut the lead to eight going into halftime.

In the second half, we continued to come back. I continued my good play by making three more shots to cut the lead to two points. We completed the full comeback and beat the Celtics by two points. After the games, we all shook hands and the Celtics players said they had us on the ropes until we took over the game. They congratulated us, and we all were very happy for the success of our first neighborhood basketball league.

Defining Moments

The next year, the summer of 1986, had many defining events that would aff ect my life. I was due to graduate from college in the spring semester. There would be an outside addition to the league. I would meet a young lady who would change my life.

In the summer of 1986, I was playing with a fire hydrant with my niece. Her friend was sitting nearby, beautiful and dry. She didn't want to get wet from the fire hydrant. I went over, picked her up, and put her into the water. She was not happy with me. She asked my niece my name, age, and what I do. I also asked who she was. Her name was Shanice and she was a few years younger than me. I had reservations about getting involved with a young lady more than two years younger than me, but I liked her. She was a senior in high school and I would soon be a senior in college. We struck up a conversation and decided to go out on a date. Throughout the summer we spent a lot of time together and became very fond of each other. We were together all the time going to the movies and to dinner or to an amusement park. We had become a couple. We talked on the phone all hours of the night.

Leading up to my graduation in the spring of 1987, I was very happy with the way things were going in my life. I was working a full-time job and a part-time job. I was attending college and about to graduate, and I was involved in a relationship. I didn't have much time to do anything else. My schedule was as busy as they come.

May came faster than I expected. On the day I was to get my degree, I was very happy, not just for myself but for my mother, who would have two sons graduate from college. Many of the people I loved would attend my graduation and they were planning a small get together once I got back home. Most of my neighborhood friends were invited. They all congratulated me. My girlfriend Shanice showed up, but she didn't want to go outside in the yard to celebrate. I asked her why. She said she didn't want to off end anyone. I asked her who would she be off ending. She said one of my friends, Dave, liked her and she didn't want to off end him by being there. I thought this was odd and I convinced her that she was my girlfriend and she would not be off ending anyone. She joined the celebration and we all had a good time, but this situation would present itself more clearly in the future.

For graduation, I wanted to do something special for both of us. I contacted a travel agency and made reservations to fly to Nassau, Bahamas and vacation for one week. We had a good time in the Bahamas. We got into several arguments, because I wanted to get out and do things and she wanted to stay in the hotel. I didn't know then what was wrong with her, but I found out once we got back from the Bahamas. As the summer approached, there would be more changes.

Transitioning

Once we returned from the Bahamas, Shanice sat me down and she said she had something very important to tell me. I was prepared for the news. She was pregnant. I wasn't really shocked. I knew we were practicing safe sex, but not one hundred percent. She looked worried, as if she thought I would say something negative. It was far from what I was thinking. With the biggest smile ever, I said, "This is the best news I have heard in a long time." I was going to become a father. It changed everything about the path I was on. I still wanted to become a professional basketball player, but this changed everything. I now only wanted to take care of my girlfriend and my child. I started thinking about how I was going to do this. I had just graduated from college and I didn't have a job. But I knew I would do something. I decided to join the Armed Forces.

 NEVER RUN AWAY FROM THE RESPONSIBILITIES THAT ACCOMPANY YOUR CHOICES.

I contacted a recruiter and proceeded to take the ASVAB test for entry into the service. I didn't score high enough to get into the branch I wanted to, which was the Air Force. I scored high enough to join the Army, but I didn't want to join the Army. Many of my relatives had joined the Army and I wanted to be diff erent by joining the Air Force. The recruiter suggested I study the ARCO books. I was still working at the library for the summer and Mrs. Rather allowed me to study if there wasn't too much going on during the day. I studied every day for a month and it was time to re-take the test. This time I scored well enough to join the Air Force. I was so happy and I just kept the good news to myself.

The transition would be swift. I was scheduled to go to boot camp on August 17, 1987 and it was already June of that year. After two weeks, I decided to tell my mother and then I would tell Shanice. I sat my mother down and I explained to her that I had joined the Air Force. I also told her that Shanice was pregnant. Ma knew she was pregnant. Mother's instinct, I guess. She asked why I wanted to join the Air Force. I told her I have a child to care for, and I saw this as an opportunity to do just that. Ma was very supportive.

I told Shanice of my plans. She was concerned about me not being there. I told her of my intentions to care for all three of us and asked her to be patient with me. I then laid out the plans I had for the both of us. I told her I would go away to boot camp. When I got my permanent station, I would send for her and the baby. The baby was due in January 1988. I was due to complete basic training and technical school by the end of November 1987. There were still many things to go through and with everything happening so fast, the one place I could find peace was on the basketball court.

We let an outside team into the Pigtown basketball league. The summer league started at the beginning of June 1987 and it would end August 1987. The team we let into the League was called the Lions Club. The team was made up of very good, savvy players and they were much more experienced than the players on my team, except for my friend Darrin and myself. The league went well. There was no real dominate team. Our team, the 76ers, ended with the league's best record by one game over the rival Celtics & the Lions Club. Both teams finished with the same record. When the playoff started, the Celtics were paired against the Lions Club. My team was hoping the Celtics would beat the Lions Club. This did not happen. The Lions Club beat the Celtics in a nail bitter. It was a very intense struggle between both teams.

We beat the other playoff team, the Lakers, to advance to the best of three Championship series with the Lions Club. The Lions Club used good shooting and intimidation to take game one. They beat us convincingly and my team of young players were very dejected and distraught. I called a meeting with my team and explained that this was only one game and we could still win this series. We were the favorite team and we had the whole neighborhood backing us. I looked into their eyes and could tell they didn't believe what I was saying. I decided to lead by example. I had a very good second game. I scored twenty-five points and we won by two points. It helped to restore confidence in my team.

The third game was a dog fight. Neither team led by as many as two points. The games came down to one shot. At the end of the game, I designed a play to have Darrin start at the foul line elbow on the left side. He would then curl down at the basket off a pick set by Marcus Turner. If Darrin was not open, then the ball would go to Marcus Turner or once I passed the ball in, it would come back to me for the shot. Darrin was not open off the pick, but he kept curling and coming towards me on the elbow of the right foul line. I passed him the ball and he shot the ball with two seconds on the clock. It seemed the ball was in the air for a half hour. The ball went through the nets, and the whole neighborhood swarmed the court to hug Darrin. We defeated the Lions Club. We went over and shook their hands to congratulate them for a great series.

Chapter 4

AFTER COLLEGE - JOINING THE AIR FORCE

"Hold still. Stay there. Tease back the layers. You are in the space between your comfort zone and infinity. You want to hide. Not be seen. Not be open. Not be vulnerable. But you have to. There are two ways to do this—soft and gentle or fast and hard. Both will get you to the other side, if you let them."

~ JEANETTE LEBLANC

B asic training was a very trying time for me, but it was also exciting. The first day I left for basic training was very intense. I was at the MEPS station all day long and I had reservations. I was thinking of not joining the Air Force after all. Then, finally, I took my physical and they drove us out to the airport to get on the airplane.

> THE FIRST STEP IN ANY NEW DIRECTION IS ALWAYS THE HARDEST TO TAKE. MANY WILL TURN AND GO THE OTHER WAY. YOU DON'T HAVE TO.

Basic training was in San Antonio, Texas at Lackland Air Force Base. I remember my first day getting off the plane. It was 6 PM and it had just begun to get dark. We got off the bus and several men in smoky hats were yelling and screaming at us. I had no idea what I had gotten myself into.

The first night was rough. We all wondered what was going to happen next. We had all types of races in our group, ages 17 to 36. The next morning, we were awakened at 5 AM with more yelling and screaming. I was a little older than many of the guys who had joined the air force and I knew all the yelling and mind games were to weed out those who were not worthy of joining the Air Force. The first few days we walked around in our civilian clothes. We went to diff erent places for diff erent things, for example, to get our uniforms, medical shots, classes, and back and forth to the cafeteria for breakfast, lunch, and dinner.

> THE GREATEST AMONG US ARE THOSE WHO ARE NOT DETERRED BY DISCOURAGEMENT OR DIFFICULTIES. THEY STAY THE COURSE, NOT MATTER HOW HARD IT GETS.

After a few days, we were all assigned separate duties to keep the dormitory clean and neat. I was assigned as a bed liner. Our Technical Instructor's (TI) name was SSgt. Lauren.

SSgt. Lauren was about 5' 9" and 165 pounds. He yelled all the time, and he did not like for us to mess up at anything we did. He was always in competition with the other TIs.

The Day Room

Each evening, we all met in the day room to discuss what happened that day and the schedule for the next day. We also received any mail sent to us by loved ones.

The dormitory was set up with four lines of beds in a two-bay area. We had four squad leaders and one dorm chief. The dorm chief was responsible for keeping all of us in line while the TI wasn't around. The squad leaders were responsible for reporting anything done wrong by the squad they were in charge of. They reported this information to the dorm chief, and the dorm chief reported it to the TI.

The first week of training passed with much ease as we began to learn what to do and what not to do. During the second week, we received our uniforms and went to class. We learned how to be a dorm guard.

Dorm Guard Duty

Dorm Guard duty was always intense because you never knew what to expect. The TIs came in all hours of the day and night and tried to enter the buildings any way they could. If you got tripped up, you could be sent back a day or two, or a week.

During training, our day was filled with appointments all day until 1500 hours. After 1500, many of the TIs went home and we had some down time to ourselves in the evening. During this time, many friendships were formed.

Flight 851

I once knew everyone who was in Flight 851. I will share some stories that stand out in my mind. I will start with C.W.

C.W. was my closest friend while in basic training because he was the closest to my age and he was one of the four tallest individuals in the flight, myself being one. Because of his height, he was always getting singled out by the TI. If there was anything the TI saw C.W. doing wrong, he would go over to C.W. and stand in front of him, look him in the eye, and start yelling at him. One night C.W. woke me up. He said, "Moe, I need to talk with you. I am so tired of this shit." We were two weeks from completing training. C.W. was planning to confront the TI in the morning and kick his ass, and then go back to California. I told him he had come too far and there were only two weeks left. I told him to speak with the TI before deciding to kick his ass.

The next day SSgt. Lauren showed up and C.W. told him in a loud voice that he wanted to speak with him. SSgt. Lauren invited him to his office. They were in the office for thirty minutes. C.W. emerged from the office with nothing to say, but the look he had when he went into the office had changed. He looked more calm and relaxed. I figured I would leave him alone and he would tell me what happen when he felt like it.

At the end of the training day, after all the TIs were gone, C.W. came over to my bay area and began to tell me what happened in his meeting with SSgt. Lauren. He said he asked SSgt. Lauren why he was always singling him out and picking on him. He said SSgt. Lauren then said, "C.W. you are the tallest person in the flight and if all your flight members see me getting on you and keeping you in line, then they will all follow suit. I don't want you to take this personal, but this is why I do it." C.W. said he understood and the meeting was over.

 IT IS NOT THE WORSE PEOPLE THAT GET SINGLED OUT AND PICKED ON, BUT THOSE WHO DEMONSTRATE THE GREATEST POTENTIAL.

In the coming weeks, SSgt. Lauren and C.W. got along much better. The TI had demoted one of the dorm chiefs after one week. SSgt. Lauren searched all of us to find who would make a good dorm chief. One of the first things you learn about the military is this, you don't volunteer for anything. SSgt. Lauren selected Airman Schott, but he did not want the position and was reluctant to take on the responsibility. After some convincing by SSgt. Lauren, Airman Schott agreed to become the new dorm chief.

Airman Schott was very young, age 17, and he lacked patience and direction. One evening while it was quiet, I explained to him that as a leader, he must be able to gain the respect of those he leads by setting the example. He needed to be stern when needed, compassionate when needed, disciplinary when needed, and congratulatory when needed. A leader does not assign tasks that he would not do himself. In the beginning, Airman Schott just yelled at his fellow airmen when they did something wrong or if a situation did not go well. In the weeks following our talk, I started to see a change in Airman Schott. He began to do more of the things I had suggested and, at the end of training, he had all the skills of a good leader.

 YOU CAN ONLY REPRODUCE IN OTHERS QUALITIES THAT YOU YOURSELF POSSESS.

The next person I remember is Airman Tent (not his real name). During our first night in boot camp, we were up until 10 PM, just sharing stories of how we got to the point we were at, and why we joined the Air Force. While I was asleep, I was awakened early in the night and I looked over to the bed next to me and I could see the blanket in a tent form. I wiped my eyes to get a better look and then it dawned on me that the guy in the bed next to me was dreaming of someone and he had an erection that made his blanket look like a tent. When we woke up the next morning, I said to Airman Tent, "Whatever it is you got going over there in your bed, you make sure you keep that shit over there in your bed."

Then there was Airman Johnson, who was a bit different from everyone else. He was very good at drawing, but he didn't seem to be a normal guy. This was not a bad thing, he was just different. The story leaked that he was not supposed to be in the Air Force because he was a sleep walker.

One night we all woke up to find Airman Johnson sleep walking. He went directly to the bed of the third squad leader, Airman Harlbaugh. And they didn't get along. Airman Harlbaugh got out of his bed and stood up, and Airman

Johnson punched him in his face. Harlbaugh was so angry. He was about to wake Johnson up, and not in a civilized manner, but everyone grabbed him. Medics say you are not supposed to wake a person who is sleep walking, because of medical reasons. Airman Johnson then turned around and walked back to his bunk, laid down, and went back to sleep. The next morning, he claimed he had no memory of the incident.

I remember a young man assigned the duty of Fire Marshall and taking out the trash. One night, while we were asleep (everything seemed to happen at night), the Fire Marshall woke up screaming at the top of his lungs, "I don't want to take out the trash anymore and I don't want to be the Fire Marshall." He woke us all up. We told him to shut up and go back to sleep.

I remember Airman Serino, the dorm guard monitor. He was responsible for scheduling guard duty. I remember Serino because of the look he gave me the first day of training. I didn't think much of it at the time. It became clear later why he looked at me that way.

I became close friends with Airman Jackson during boot camp. One night, while he was performing dorm guard duty at our dormitory, He tapped me on the shoulder at my bunk. He was already in his underwear and he said, "Moe, you had better hurry up and get out to the dorm guard stand. There is no one out there." You are supposed to give the next person for dorm guard duty a fifteen-minute notice before shift change. I didn't have any clothes on. I hurried, and I could do my shift without any problems. Dorm Guard duty was for two hours and most airmen liked to perform their shift in the wee hours, because this was the time everything was quiet.

My bunk was next to Serino and I always got him to schedule me for the wee hours. During my time performing dorm guard duty, all I thought about was how I could get back at Jackson for what he had done to me. Then it came to me. I had the perfect plan.

During Dorm Guard duty, the TIs always pulled stunts to trip up airmen to get them washed back a week or two. There was this one TI that had built a reputation for washing airman back. His dormitory was right above our dormitory. My bunk was next to the dorm guard monitor. I said to Serino, "Give Jackson two hours of duty at the dorm right above us." Serino asked why. No one liked to perform duty at that dormitory. I told him that Jackson wanted to see what it felt like.

Serino agreed and filled out the schedule and posted it where he usually did. Airman Jackson looked at the schedule and he said to Serino, "Hey man, why you put me on the schedule for the dorm above us?" He was pacing back and forth. Serino said to him, "I cannot change it now. You are scheduled to be there in one and a half hour." I heard all this and I was just smiling. Jackson finally accepted the schedule and he left to perform his duty.

After two hours of duty, Jackson returned and he was animated. He went on and on about how the TI tried to wash him back with different stunts. He said to Serino, "Please don't schedule me for that dorm anymore. Why did you schedule me for that dorm anyway?" Serino then said, "Moe told me you wanted to perform guard duty above our dorm." Jackson asked me about it, and I was laughing hysterically. When I managed to stop laughing, I said, "The next time you come to me to replace you on guard duty, you had better be in your uniform." I think he got the message.

The final story that comes to mind is about a young man whose name I do not remember. We will call him John. John's bunk was two bunks over from mine. At nights, I would sing or hum a few tunes and the guys would listen. It was usually a good time for us because everyone was settling down and you could have some good conversation with your fellow airman.

John's story began during the second week of basic training when he received his first letter from his girlfriend. In the letter she wrote, "Dear John. I miss you so much and I cannot wait to see you again. Please hurry and come home. I miss you so much and I love you." The third week John received another letter and his girlfriend wrote, "Dear John. It has been several weeks now since you have been gone. I talked with your friend Daniel and we both ---." You can guess how that story ended.

Blue Line Inspection

As we moved further into our training, we became more knowledgeable of what was expected of us individually and as a group. We were into our fourth week and it was time for our blue line inspection, which involved inspecting our wall lockers and how we looked in our full-dress uniforms. SSgt. Lauren's inspections were known to be difficult to pass. He often told us that no one usually passed his blue line inspection on the first round.

On the day of our inspections, we were all inspected at 10 AM. SSgt. Lauren explained that we would know the results later, at the end of the day.

At the end of the day, SSgt. Lauren went over all the inspections and call each of us in alphabetical order to tell us how we had done. My last name begins with the letter M and I didn't like the waiting and anticipation to find out how I had done. When he got to my name, Airman Sturgell was the only person who had passed.

Finally, he called me into his office and pointed out some things that were wrong with my inspection. He told me I had failed. I had the same look on my face as all the other airmen who had failed. I went back to my bunk and checked for all the things SSgt. Lauren mentioned was wrong with my inspection. It wasn't quite adding up. Everyone was working on their uniforms and their wall lockers. After about a half hour, SSgt. Lauren called me back to his office and he said, "I don't believe it. I was just double checking the inspections and it looks like you passed." He then told me to get the hell out of his office and go down stairs to the canteen area for some down time.

Going to the canteen was very rewarding to everyone, because you could catch a bit of a break from the TIs and make phone calls home. Also, passing the blue line inspection was significant because it was the last inspection one had to pass. Once you passed the blue line inspection, you only had one more week until graduation. It was like a great big weight had been lifted and I was so happy. I went down to the canteen to call my mother and Shanice to tell them the good news.

Trouble at Home

Shanice had moved in with my Mother and she was sleeping in my bed. During this time, I was receiving letters from my mother and my girlfriend and they could not get along. My mother allowed Shanice to stay at her house out of kindness for her son. Shanice wrote to tell me that my mother was difficult to live with and stayed up all hours of the night listening to music. Back and forth it would go during the time I was in basic training. Ma wrote, "Her ass has to go. I can no longer put up with someone trying to tell me how to live in my own house." I started thinking, I have a man in a smoky hat screaming at me every morning, trying to prepare me for war, but the war is back at the house where I grew up.

One day, we were in the day room at the end of the day, and SSgt. Lauren passed out the mail as he usually did. I had started getting four to five letters a day from my friends. That day I received a bulky letter from Shanice. I tried to put it away, but SSgt. Lauren insisted on knowing what was in the letter. I opened it and there was a small baby shirt inside. SSgt. Lauren said with a nice laugh, "It looks like you may have hit it one too many times and you are going to be a daddy." Everyone congratulated me.

We were nearing the end of our six weeks of training, and everyone was anxious to move on to their next assignment or station.

I want to share one more story I remember about my six weeks at Lackland AFB, about Airman Forbes. He was great at any task once he learned how to do it. The problem was getting him to the point of knowing how to do it. Forbes sometimes had problems in basic training, for example, marching, shooting, and completing assignments. During the last week of training, SSgt. Lauren and a few of his friends decided to play the prank of a lifetime on Forbes. Forbes was always having problems marching. SSgt. Lauren explained to him that if he didn't get better at marching and pass our final test, he was going to wash Forbes back to the first week of training. Forbes told us about it and we all rallied around him to help him with his marching.

We felt confident that, with our help, he would pass along with the rest of us.

Finally, the time came to take our marching test. I must say I wasn't a great marcher either, and I was nervous also. SSgt. Lauren tested four airmen at a time. When it was my turn, it seemed like it took hours to take the test. I passed and I was very much relieved. Then it was time for Forbes. SSgt. Lauren would not let anyone stand around to watch how the other airmen did during their marching test. Everyone had to go back to the dormitory and wait. When Forbes returned to the dormitory, we could see by the expression on his face that he did not do so well. When we learned that Forbes had failed, we were all dejected because he was the only one who failed. Forbes then had to clean out his wall locker. He had to put on civilian clothes and go down to the main office to sign paper work explaining why he was washed back to the first week of training.

We were all excited after passing our marching test, because we were receiving orders for our next assignment, which was Technical School. We tried to console Forbes and contain our jubilant feelings. Forbes collected all his things and he was on his way down to the office. We said goodbye and wished him good luck. Forbes completed all his paper work and he was assigned to his new Flight.

While sitting on his bunk, all the new recruits entered the dormitory with their bunk assignments. They all had this look of excitement and worry on their faces. News travels fast on a military base and within a dormitory. Forbes could hear the new recruits talking and staring at him as he sat on his bunk. Finally, one recruit was bold enough to approach Forbes. He asked Forbes if he was the airman who was washed back after completing five weeks of training. Forbes was clearly upset and told the recruit to get out of his face. At 4:30 that evening, SSgt. Lauren called to the office and explained to him that he was not washed back and that it was all a practical joke, with several of the TIs in on it. Forbes was elated that he was not washed back.

Graduation Day

We finally graduated from basic training and everyone was nervous and excited to be leaving San Antonio and moving on to the first military base and their first assignment. We all hugged and said our goodbyes. Some were leaving by plane and some were leaving by bus. I and two of my friends were leaving by bus to go to Keesler AFB in Mississippi. I was on my way to get trained as an administrative specialist. My training would be for three to four weeks. The bus ride was very long, but we were still excited to be leaving Lackland AFB.

During our briefing, once we got to Keesler, we were informed there would be fewer restrictions once we had settled in at our new base. Keesler AFB is somewhat of a blur.

I was not at the base long enough to remember much. I remember going to school early in the morning and performing dorm guard duty. I did have my own room and I wrote many letters to my friends. I often wrote Shanice and I called her also.

I spent four weeks at Keesler, because I didn't pass the typing test to bypass my first week. I had to spend that week learning to type better. Once I completed my training at Keesler, it was time to move on to my next assigned base.

When you join the military, you fill out a dream sheet, where you choose three preferred bases to start your military career. I chose any base in California, Florida, or Maryland, preferably Andrews AFB. When I received my orders, the base where I was to start my career was MacDill AFB in Tampa, Florida. I was very excited to get a warm climate base.

Before reporting to MacDill AFB, I was given leave time to go home for three weeks. I was very, very excited to be going home to see my family and my friends and to see Shanice. I didn't tell my mother or Shanice when I would be coming home. I thought I would surprise them.

In November of 1987, I caught a flight from Mississippi to Maryland. I would arrive at around 6 PM. Once I got to BWI in Maryland, I flagged down an airport taxi to take me to Baltimore. I pulled up at 1340 Cleveland Street and no one was outside. As I started to get out of the car, our next-door neighbor and a very good friend of the family, Mrs. Kimberly Johnson, recognized me. She told me how nice I looked in a uniform. I proceeded to the front door, and turned the knob at the house where I lived with my mother.

My mother and Lady were sitting at the kitchen table. My mother jumped up and said, "Oh my god, my son is home." We hugged long and hard. It was very emotional. I hugged my sister and told them both how I had missed them and the rest of the family. I then asked my mother where was Shanice. Ma said she went back home to stay with her mother.

I called Shanice and told her I was home and I was on my way to see her. When I arrived, we hugged and kissed for a long time. We were excited to see each other. I spent most my leave from the service with Shanice during the month of November. I visited some friends and family members, especially my grandmother, Mrs. Goldie Molock. I talked with my grandmother for a long time and listened to her tell stories from the past and ate some of her good ole home cooking.

The three weeks went by fast and it was time for me to move on to MacDill AFB. Shanice cried because she was not ready for me to go. I told her not to worry. I would send for her and we would get a place off base to live. I would have to get all that set up within a month or two.

My First Base

I arrived at MacDill AFB on a Friday evening, and it took me awhile to get settled in. I had all weekend to get prepared to start my Air Force career. That Saturday, I woke up with the intent to find the gym. The gym has always been a good place to meet new friends and to find out where things are on a base. I found the gym and there were many guys playing basketball. I had to sign up on a board on the wall to play.

Whenever you start to play any sport with a new set of guys, there is always a feeling of being out of process. You don't know what to expect of the new guys you are playing with and they don't know what to expect of you. Whenever I stepped out on any basketball court, I always had the confidence of knowing I could play the game at a high level. This was the case anywhere I went to play. I remember playing with guys who were not very good players. The established players all want to play together and I knew this was normal. Things were set up by design to see if I could play.

Before the game started, I introduced myself to the players I would be playing with. I only remember one player and his name was Dante. He was a small young man and he was a good ball handler, a point guard. Dante gave me a scouting report of the players we were about to face.

The game started and I made my first shot, which was a jump shot. My next shot, I drove to the basket and I made a left-hand shot. There were a few moans on the sideline as if I had done something different.

As the game went on, I scored several more baskets and I finished with nine of our thirteen points. We won the game. We went on to win three more games. By the time we got to the fifth game, I was tired and it seemed like they had stacked the team against us for this game. I figured we had won enough games and my future friends decided they had seen enough. After the games, it was customary to sit in the gym and talk about any and everything. This conversation was about me. They all wanted to know where I was from and where I would be working.

I introduced myself. Dante introduced me to all the guys and they explained where many of the important places on base were located, for example, the Commissary/BX, the chow hall, the shoppette, the personnel building, and the NCO Club. Dante then asked what dormitory I was staying in and if I needed a ride anywhere. They were all very nice and respectful to me.

One guy stood up and he was very serious about what he was about to say. He said, "It is nice to see all of us sitting around talking with each other and everyone is getting along pretty well." He then made a very bold statement. "If your wife or your girlfriend is out at the clubs in the area and she is trying to give me some play, I am going to fuck her. I am telling you now because I don't want you all getting mad at me when your wife is the one out there doing the wrong thing when she should be home with your ass." I knew right then that I would have to tell my woman to stand clear of this guy. After talking, we left the gym and Dante gave me a ride to the shoppette, where we all purchased food and some drinks. He then gave me a ride to my dorm and before I got out of the car, he asked if I would like to get off the base and come to his apartment to watch some basketball.

Dante lived off base right outside the main gate with his wife Janet. When we arrived, he introduced me to Janet and she told me to make myself at home. After about ten minutes, some of the guys who were at the gym arrived and we all sat and talked and watched the games. Dante and Janet often invited me over and they always had food and drinks to accompany my visit. It was only my second night on the base, but Dante asked if I would like to go to the NCO Club. I said yes.

When we got to the club, many of the guys we played basketball with earlier that day were there. Immediately, I felt I was the new kid on the block. Several women and guys there checked me out. They knew I was not a regular at this point. After a night at the club, Dante dropped me off at my dormitory.

On Sunday I woke up and headed for the gym. Once I got to the gym, I was greeted differently. In one day, news of a young brother who could play basketball had spread like wildfire. I was picked to play with some of the more established players this time around, and we held the court all morning into afternoon. Once again, we sat around and talked after the game and they asked where I worked. I did not know where I would be working yet. This was my first weekend.

I watched the basketball games that Sunday with Dante once again.

 YOU WILL KNOW YOU HAVE A REAL PASSION FOR SOMETHING, WHEN NO MATTER HOW FAR YOU GO, IT ALWAYS SEEMS TO FOLLOW YOU AROUND.

On Monday, I had orders to report to the Headquarters building in dress blue uniform to find out where I would be working. When I got to the Headquarters building, I was greeted by Master Sgt. Mitch. He said they had a desk job in another building waiting for me, but the person holding the job hadn't left yet. He wanted me to work in the Base Information Transfer Center (BITC). I had no idea what the BITC was. Mitch walked me around to the BITC and introduced me to everyone in the center. There were five guys and one female running the BITC. All were Caucasians. The female's name was Irene Foreman. There was an immediate diff erence at BITC once I arrived. I was only supposed to be there for a short period of time because I was going to be moved to a diff erent office. I took an immediate liking to Irene.

In a short span of time, we became very good friends and enjoyed each other's company.

After several weeks, I became more familiar with the job and began to like it very much. A guy in the shop named Rob was getting out of the Air Force. This opened the door for me to have a permanent position in the BITC. They were still going to move me if I wanted, but I had grown very fond of Irene and I was getting along well with the guys. Irene and I talked about the idea of me moving on. I told her I wanted to stay at BITC.

Chapter 5

BITC

We must become bigger than we have been: more courageous, greater in spirit, larger in outlook. We must become members of a new race, overcoming petty prejudice, owing our ultimate allegiance not to nations but to our fellow men within the human community.

~ HAILE SELASSIE

My time at BITC was wonderful. I found a great friend in Irene and I had a great job. We delivered the mail all across the base and I got a chance to meet everyone. It was great.

 FAVOR PRECEDES PASSION.

I only had one incident while I was in BITC that may be considered negative. One day I came back from lunch a little late and the whole gang was in the back of the office. I could hear them talking about me, so I stayed out front to hear what they had to say. They were discussing having a black guy work with them, and they were discussing likes and dislikes. Some of them had never worked with a black guy before. They talked about the things I did, and didn't do, everything they would not have spoken to me about in person. I could hear Irene defending me. Towards the end of their discussion, I decided to walk in the back. I will never forget the looks on their faces. It was obvious they were just talking about me. I told them that if they had a problem with me or had questions, they should not talk behind my back. They should come to me and I would answer all their questions. From that point on I did not have any problems in BITC and we all got along great.

During my stay at MacDill AFB and working in the BITC, I learned many things and once received Employee of the Quarter. While at MacDill, we played basketball all the time. We played Monday through Thursday and Saturday and Sunday. As I made more friends and became more comfortable with my surroundings, I became known as one of the top players on the base. We went into the inner city and played against some very tough competition.

One time we played in the inner city, where we were all recognized as the Air Force boys. One of my friends, Kermit Beasley, had played on the court before and was picked to play right off the bat. This left me and my other three friends with the winners for next game. While we were waiting, one of the guys from the neighborhood came down to the court and asked who has the next winners. I told him I did. He said he was taking my winners. Not knowing the area or the people in the area, I just looked at him and told him to take the winners. As luck would have it, he was picked up to replace a guy who had gotten hurt while playing. This guy was about six feet four inches tall and weighed over 250 pounds.

The game went on after the injury to the player, and the team with the guy who wanted to take my winners won. I was hoping his team would win, because there is more than one way to skin a cat. It was now our chance to play and I was salivating over the chance to play against this guy. All the games went to thirteen points by one. I made my first shot and proceeded to make my next nine shots. All of them were against this guy. After the first shot, he said that was just luck. I hit the next three and he realized that I was a match for him. When I made the next five shots, the crowd was talking and the guy didn't have anything else to say. My friends who I came with were all smiling.

 SOMETIMES THE BEST WAY TO PROVE YOURSELF IS NOT BY SAYING ANYTHING, BUT DOING WHAT YOU DO BEST.

The guy came over to me after the game and said, "Good game." He really wasn't going to take my winners, and he had no idea I could play so well. He invited us all to a cookout he was having later that day, and he wanted me to meet his sister. We all exchanged numbers and from that time, they would come out to the base and play ball with us.

As my career in the Air Force started to develop, I became one of the top intermural players on the base. I averaged about twenty-five points per game. Our team was always undersized and out maned, but we always competed and were never blown out. We just never made it to the championship.

In one game we competed against the Security Forces Team, and their team was good. We were in first place and this was a big game for us because they were our primary competition in our division. Two minutes into the game, I was tossed out because the referee smelled alcohol on my breath. Before the game, we had celebrated my supervisor's birthday by having one beer with her. The referee was a Security Forces member. We lost the game by twenty points. I apologized to my team for what had happened.

Making the AFB Team

After intermural came the tryouts for the MacDill AFB Team. This was a big deal on the base because the team would travel and play against the community colleges in the area, the CBA teams, and the other military bases in the area. After tryouts, I made the team and was named Captain.

Before we played our first game, we were invited to play in a three on three tournament in downtown Tampa. It would be four of us playing in the tournament: Kermit, Ronnie, Myself and Smitty. The game would finish at twenty-two points or fifteen minutes, whichever came first. You had to win three games to make it to the championship game.

We won our first game by two points and the second by eight points, but the third game was a battle against a good team. We won by one point. We made it to the Championship Game and by this time we were known as the Air Force Boys.

We would go up against the defending Champions. The winner would go to Texas to play in the Nationals.

The Champs had a four-man team consisting of very accomplished players from the area. One player was a previous professional drafted by the Philadelphia 76ers. It was a very close game, a nip and tuck. Neither team led by more than one point at a time. There were plays where the Champs tried to intimidate our team, but we didn't back down at all. I was having a good game and made several shots, missing only one out of five. The score was 21 to 20 and the 15 minutes was about to run out. Ronnie had the ball in the left-hand corner. I was hot, and all we needed was one two-pointer to win the game. Everybody was cheering for Ronnie to pass me the ball, because I was open at the two-point line. Ronnie took the shot and missed. We lost the game. He apologized for not passing the ball.

The MacDill Base Team was named the AF Falcons. We would go on to play other military bases, junior colleges in the area, and CBA Continental Basketball Association teams. We played teams such as the Naval Air Station in Jacksonville, Florida. We played all the military bases in the area: Tyndall AFB, Patrick AFB, Eglin AFB, Homestead AFB, and Moody AFB. We played against Hurburt Field, and Mayport Naval Station.

We also played against Hillsborough Community College at least once a week and all the games were competitive. We only beat them once. We had a better record against the other bases. One weekend we played Patrick AFB on a Saturday evening and then played them again on Sunday afternoon. In the first, I had a very good game. I scored 35 points and we won by 10 points. We saw many of Patrick's players later that evening at the NCO Club. When I walked into the Club, I could hear whispers. We all talked and became friends. I congratulated several of their players, and they returned the compliment. One guy said, "Man, you were making shots from everywhere, but that will not happen at Patrick." I said, "We will see."

The second game was more competitive. Patrick AFB Base had a very good player. Patrick played a box in one to stop me from scoring. It worked for much of the game. There was a different player guarding me every five minutes. Patrick had a sizeable lead with five minutes to play. They were leading by 15 points. I was able to make five straight three pointers to tie the game. We won the game in overtime by two points.

The next game I remember is the game we played at Mayport Naval Station. The military always gets paid on the first and the fifteenth. I didn't get a chance to purchase a new pair of basketball shoes and we were taking our travel bus to play at Mayport on the first of the month. I had to wear some old basketball shoes that I had been wearing regularly at our gym.

When we got to Mayport and I stepped out on the court, I was immediately heckled by the fans for not getting new shoes. My shoes were old and not in sync with my other teammates. The game began and once again I had a good game. I scored thirty points, but we lost. As I was leaving the court, I realized I had gained the respect of the fans. One of the female fans said, "Alright number 23, we see that you got game, but next time get some new shoes."

After playing the Naval Air Station team, the next weekend we were scheduled to play a professional team, the Florida Sun. During the week leading up to the game, Captain Johnson asked if I was interested in being the Captain of the team. He said I was a natural leader and the rest of the guys respond to my leadership on and off the court. The weekend came fast. We rode the MacDill AFB Bus to play the Florida Sun. When we got to the arena, it was more like a gym than an arena. There were scouts checking out the players on the professional team. The Sun had about twenty guys on their team and we had only eight. The format of the game was different also. We were used to playing two halves, but the professionals played four quarters. The game started and the Sun won the Sun. We played well the first quarter and only trailed by one point at the end.

The second quarter began. It was obvious at this point that it would be a long game for us because we were already tired from the intense play. At the half, we trailed by four points and were feeling pretty good about our efforts.

Once the third quarter began, it was pretty apparent we were tired. The Sun took a fifteen-point commanding lead in the third period and raised the lead to twenty in the final period. I played okay, but I thought I could have played a lot better. I was four for twelve shooting and it didn't sit well with me. When it was apparent we were going to lose, I stood near one of the guys from the other team who said to me, "You guys probably play basketball maybe once a week or mostly on weekends." He was right. They beat us bad that day. He said, "Well, we had a lot more bodies than you guys." He continued, "Look at who is on our team. There is World B. Free, a former NBA player trying to get back to the league. There is Keith Lee, Larry Bird's brother. My point is this, you guys just play the game for fun, these guys are playing the game for keeps because they have families to feed. This is their livelihood and their jobs. So, don't feel disappointed. You guys played well." That helped to put things into proper perspective for me. Their coach came over to chat with me. He said, "I like the way you play and I think you have a nice game. How would you like to try out for the team and maybe play professionally?" I was happy the coach recognized me, though I thought I played terribly in that game. He said, "How long do you have on your enlistment?" I told him two years. He said, "That is a problem. I have to cut my roster to fifteen by the end of the week and you are still obligated to the military." It was nice to be noticed. Who knows what would have happened had I taken on that opportunity.

 SOME OPPORTUNITIES WILL COME ALONG ONLY ONCE IN THIS LIFETIME, AND THEY COME SO SUBTLY, YOU MIGHT NOT EVEN RECOGNIZE THEM UNTIL THEY HAVE PASSED.

We got on the bus and headed back to MacDill AFB. One of my teammates asked me what the coach and I was talking about. I told him. We both agreed my enlistment would be a problem. My teammate said, "You can always try to get orders to go overseas."

They treat you like NBA stars overseas when you play for the base team. I hear some of the guys there play basketball as their job. I thought that was great news and decided I would put in for orders right away, but part of me thought the dream of becoming an NBA player had started to fade and I needed to concentrate more on my military career. I was 26 years old and not many guys make it to the NBA after a certain age.

I had to contend with the idea of telling Irene I was going to put in orders to go overseas. I thought this would be a good opportunity for me. The game with the Sun was on a Saturday, so I had the rest of Saturday and Sunday to decide how I was going to tell Irene. This was a tough decision for me, because Irene and I had grown to be very close friends.

Chapter 6

THAT'S TOO MUCH ROOM

You should never view your challenges as a disadvantage. Instead, it's important for you to understand that your experience facing and overcoming adversity is actually one of your biggest advantages.

~ Michelle Obama

Shanice and Aaron had been living with me for over two years and it was going well at first. We were getting along pretty good and had made many friends. Shanice liked going to the NCO Club. This became an issue once she wanted to go to the club every weekend. In the beginning, I thought it was a good idea because she was home with Aaron all week and this was her time to get out and have some fun. Sometimes, I would go to the club by myself or we would go together once we found a babysitter.

After the game with the Florida Sun, a lot of my teammates and I went to the NCO Club. We talked about the game and what we could have done better. We all agreed we were undersized and out manned. I'd had a couple of beers. After the Club closed, I was on my way home, driving down this long stretch of road. An oncoming car crossed over into my lane and I swerved. I ended up on someone's front lawn and I had totaled our Nissan Sentra. I walked the rest of the way to my house. I wasn't hurt, but I was in tears because I had just wrecked our transportation.

When I told Shanice what had happened, she said, "What are we going to do for transportation?" Then she asked if I was okay. The fact that we didn't have transportation would become a huge problem moving forward.

The following Monday, I asked Irene about overseas assignments. She said she once did an overseas assignment and it was nice. I told her I wanted to apply for an overseas assignment because some of the guys I play ball with said this would be a great opportunity. She said I should go ahead and do what I thought was best for me. I thought she would try to convince me not to go. She did ask about Shanice and Aaron. That was my only problem.

I applied for an overseas assignment but it never went through. My home life became difficult because of the transportation issue. I had coworkers picking me up in the morning to get to work, but Shanice kept asking what we were going to do about transportation. We talked about the best option for our situation and both decided it would be best for her to go home to Baltimore for a while, so I purchased a bus ticket for them.

I felt lonely. I missed my family. The idea of playing professional basketball started to fade even more. I still played on the base team and with guys throughout the week.

The basketball court was my sanctuary, and during this time I started using the phrase "That's Too Much Room." The phrase referred to other players giving me too much room to get my shot off and get a good look at the basket. I had a very good support crew. I started talking with Irene more and she would come get me sometimes to get me out of the house. I enjoyed spending time with Irene. We always had good conversations. I was fortunate to have a friend like her.

When I called my mother, she would always say her catch line, "And this too will come to pass." I also talked with my best friend, Gwenn Oliver, and she always gave me good advice. I was also having conversations with Karen Spruill. She was another one of my friends from College. I kept in touch with Renae Sparks, my college girlfriend.

I called Shanice from time to time to ask if she was coming back to Tampa. She would say yes, with reservations. It was a year before she came back and many things changed by this time. I had friends on the base asking if she was going to come back. I had female friends asking me out to dinner or a movie. I was holding out thinking that Shanice would be back at some time. During this period, I found solitude in playing basketball. Playing relieved the stress going on in my life. Sometimes after the games, the guys asked if Shanice was coming back.

After several months, I finally secured a brown Honda Accord and enough leave time to go back to Baltimore for two weeks. It took about sixteen hours to drive from Tampa, FL to Baltimore, MD. After playing basketball with the guys for a few hours, I headed for Baltimore one Saturday afternoon.

When I arrived, I was happy to see my mother and my family. I was looking forward to seeing Shanice and Aaron. I contacted Shanice thinking she would be looking forward to seeing me also. I found out she was working and she didn't get off until 5pm. I told her I would pick her up.

When I picked Shanice up from work, she didn't seem all that happy to see me. She had me drive to her mother's house to see Aaron. I was so happy to see my little man. I asked Shanice if she would be coming back with me. She said, "I don't know." I was somewhat hurt by this. During the rest of my vacation time, I didn't see much of Shanice because she was working. But I spent time with Aaron, when time permitted. I drove around to see many of my friends and relatives while I was home. I got a chance to see Gwenn and Karen. I stopped by Renae's house, but she wasn't home. The time went quickly and it was time for me to go back to Tampa. My sister Trevia decided to go back to Tampa with me, along with her two boys, Brandon and Forrest. I tried contacting Shanice all day with no luck. I decided to go to her mother's house to see if she was there. When I got there, the only one there was her brother, Ron, but he had no idea where she was. That's when I found out she wasn't living with her mother. After much persuading, Ron took me to where she lived. I asked her if she was going back to Tampa with me. She said, "No." I told her I was taking my son. She didn't object. Shanice was living in an apartment and she was not the only one living there. I decided to leave it alone. I knew she was living with a guy. I got in the car to drive back to my mother's house to get some rest before the long ride home. Aaron was with me. While in the car, Ron said to me, "You know, she lives there with Devin Burnwood." All I said was, "I guess that is what she wants. I hope she is happy."

The next morning, I gathered Aaron and my sister and her two kids and we headed for Tampa, Florida. It was a long ride, but it was smooth and we made it in good time. We got in Sunday evening and I had to be at work the next day. My sister watched Aaron for the week she was there. I knew I would need to make other arrangements when she was gone.

The next day when I got to work, Shanice called to ask why I didn't stop by her to pick her up and why I left without her. I reminded her that she said she didn't want to go back to Tampa. I told her I knew she was living with Devin Burnwood. She hung up.

It was nice to have my sister with me for a while. She stayed for a week and then she caught the bus back to Baltimore. I told her to call me when she got home. She said she enjoyed her stay in Tampa, but she was ready to go home.

1990 was a long year. I was in constant talks with my supporting family and friends and learned a lot about myself and what I wanted to do about my relationship with Shanice. I secured daycare services through my friend, Singleton, who I played basketball with. His wife was a daycare provider and this would prove to be a blessing, because she charged me a rate I could aff ord and was nice enough to give me credit when I could not pay. This was comforting to know.

Friends kept asking me if Shanice was coming back, and I told them yes, though I was not sure. Whenever I asked her, she would tell me yes. Irene spent more time with me to take my mind off things and I will always love her for the support she gave during this time. I could call and talk with Gwenn often and she always had words of comfort for me. One conversation really sticks out. I was talking with Gwenn about how Shanice thought I had some very loyal friends and that it was nice that I kept in touch with them. She said that Devin Burnwood was her closest friend and that was who she liked to keep in touch with. I didn't know she was going to move in with him. Gwen told me Shanice was going to sleep with him and she probably already has. The thought crossed my mind but I didn't want to think about it. I would talk with my mother and she was always supportive and worried about me.

As time passed, I was starting to feel better. I settled into my daily routine, which consisted of dropping Aaron off at the daycare provider, going to work, and then picking Aaron up. Sometimes Singleton's wife kept Aaron a little longer so I could play basketball This was great. Karen would say, "I don't know why you are going through this. You don't deserve this, you are too nice of a guy." All my conversations were centered around five people, and one would prove to be the most important in my life: Renae Sparks. We talked often. I talked to her at work and through letters. I talked with Renae so much, it took my mind off many of the things I was going through.

Several months had passed and I hadn't heard from Shanice. She called me at work once in a while to check on how Aaron and I were doing. I started talking with Renae more often. Several months had passed and the idea of getting custody of Aaron popped into my head. I thought if Shanice wasn't coming back, I should look at moving forward and try to do what was best for me and Aaron. Even if I couldn't get custody, I would be able to say I tried. My circle of friends was very supportive during this ordeal. I decided to get a lawyer to advise me and speak on my behalf. I don't remember the lawyer's name, but he advised me that if I was going to get custody of Aaron, I had better act fast, because the courts generally award custody to the mother. I didn't want to leave Shanice out. I thought we could have joint custody. I told the lawyer I would talk with her about the situation when she came back to Tampa.

Shanice called the day after I met with the lawyer. She was ready to come back to Tampa. I didn't know what to expect, but I said okay. During her period of absence, several women showed interest; some wanted to cook for me or come over and spend the night. Some of them knew Shanice from the club. I talked with my circle of friends and they all said a woman recognizes a good man when they see one. Shanice said she would catch the bus back to Tampa and would leave on a Thursday. I felt good about her return but I was not excited. Thursday and Friday came and went, but Shanice did not show up. It didn't take that long to get to Tampa from Baltimore, and she hadn't contacted me. Saturday came and went and then I started to get worried. Finally, she contacted me and said she stopped in Jacksonville, Florida to see some girlfriends before she returned to Tampa.

She finally made it back to Tampa at about 9:30 PM Sunday. I was off ended because she had shown no sense of urgency about coming back. I went to bed. It had been months since I had seen her and I found it a bit awkward to sleep in the same bed. Since she had not seen Aaron in a while, she decided to sleep in his room. I was fine with that.

The next night she did sleep with me, but it was still awkward. It was awkward to the point that I got up at 2 AM and went out to a small park in the area for about an hour. When I came back, she asked me where I was. I told her I went for a walk. She didn't want to make love and she informed me that she had been sick and that she was not well. I wasn't sure I wanted to make love either because of the idea of her being with another man.

One evening, a collect call came in from a correctional facility from a Devin Burnwood. I accepted the call and asked what he wanted. He asked to speak with Shanice. I didn't want to get involved in whatever they had.

I came home one day and I picked up the mail. I opened the phone bill and it was $800.00. I was speechless. There were numerous calls from the correctional facility. I didn't have the money to pay the bill and the phone service was cut off. The awkwardness did not leave, it just wasn't the same with us. One day she called me at work and said she wanted to talk. When I got home, she said, "I know how we can save some money. I can file for a voucher to move down to the projects more into the city. This would make my commute to work an extra 20 minutes, when it only takes me five to ten minutes now." It would save money, but I was not prepared to move further into the city.

One day, I came home from work and she was gone. She left a note saying she found a place in the city. She had taken Aaron. I didn't know what to think or what to do. I thought I would wait a few days and she would contact me to explain, but I knew I wasn't moving to the city.

Several days passed and I hadn't heard from Shanice. I didn't have any transportation to go and see where she was living, so I asked my friend Monique to take me to the projects. Monique was the wife of one of my coworkers, Sheridan Ferrell. She knew the area because she was from Tampa. She was in the Air Force as well. Monique and I got into her car one evening after work and headed down to the projects. We drove around a little and finally found the address where Shanice was staying. I knocked on the door. I will never forget the look on her face when she saw me. She asked what I was doing there. I told her I came to see my son. There seemed to be a lot of hesitation in her conversation. We then went around the corner to a local park to talk some more. She told me she didn't want to be together anymore. I asked her what was really going on. She said she wanted to live a little. I told her I would be filing for custody of Aaron.

A few weeks passed and I hadn't heard from Shanice. One Friday, I decided I wanted to see Aaron. I got Irene to take me to the projects once again and told her to park where her car was not visible. I hadn't seen Aaron in a while, but that wasn't the only reason I went to see her. Shanice had taken my microwave when she moved out and I wanted it back. It was about dusk and I knocked on the door. Shanice was there. I asked for the microwave and to see my son. She said Aaron was upstairs. I pushed past her and headed up the stairs.

Aaron was sleeping in a made-up box bed and she had a waterbed. I was angry. I picked Aaron up and headed for the door. Shanice tried to stop me but she couldn't. I took Aaron to Irene's car and we left.

Later that night I realized I didn't have any clothes for Aaron. Irene warned me about going back to the projects. I felt like I needed to get out for a while. So I contacted Sheridan. Irene volunteered to watch Aaron.

Sheridan wanted to take me to a place called the New Lounge. We had been there before and we had a good time, but I had other things on my mind. I suggested that we go to that club down in the projects. Sheridan knew what I was thinking, so he refused. It took some convincing but I got him to go to this club.

We were at the club for about an hour before I got up to leave. I told Sheridan I would be back in ten minutes. What happened next put everything I was going through into in perspective. When I went back down to Shanice's apartment, to my surprise, I saw Devin Burnwood leaning on a tree. He must have spotted me before I spotted him. I suspected something was going on, but I could not quite put my finger on it. But I was in a different place mentally. I was calm and I had my son. If they wanted to be together, so be it. I hoped they were happy. Devin walked with me to the apartment. We knocked on the door and Shanice answered. Devin said we should both talk about this calmly. I told Shanice I was only there to get some clothes for Aaron. She gave me the clothes and I left.

When I went back to the club with the big box of toys and clothes, Sheridan was nowhere to be found. He had left me. I had no transportation and it was 2:30 in the morning. I went back to Shanice's apartment and knocked on the door. She came to the door and asked what I wanted. I told her buses had stopped running and I needed somewhere to sleep. I would leave early in the morning. She told me no. She and her man needed to sleep, and they had no idea what I would do once they were asleep. That is how I was treated, after all I had done.

I called Irene. She picked me up at 3:30 AM and took me to her house. I slept on her sofa.

Several weeks passed and the date to meet with my lawyer was fast approaching. When the date finally came, Shanice and I met with the lawyer and the lawyer informed Shanice of the procedure. He advised me to seek full custody. Shanice wanted joint custody. The lawyer said if I went after joint custody, I could walk away with nothing. I needed to get Shanice to agree to give me full custody. I spoke with her privately and told her I wanted full custody and she would get visitation rights. This way she could be with Devin, no distractions. I added that she should give Devin a try, and if it didn't work out, we could talk about getting back together. She finally agreed.

After all the papers were signed, Shanice said she wanted to come over and spend the day with me and Aaron. That day we went to the beach located a couple miles from the duplex where I lived. Shanice spent most of the time walking up and down the beach. When I asked her what was wrong, she said she wasn't sure she was making the right decision. I reminded her that she wanted to be with Devin and she was not in a position financially to care for Aaron. I represented stability. I took Shanice to the bus stop and she went home to the projects. Aaron cried. I told him it would be okay.

Basketball was still my sanctuary. I was still playing on the base team and I still played intermurals. I often took Aaron to the base gym and the guys took turns watching him while I was on the court. The end of my enlistment was fast approaching. Shanice would call me sparingly, to find out when I was getting out of the service and when I was coming home. Irene and I talked more about what I was going to do once I got out. I entertained the idea of staying in Tampa and just finding a job and continuing from there. I also kept in contact with Gwen and Karen. But I mostly kept in contact with Renae, so much so, she decided to come visit me and stay for a week. I don't remember the exact month, but Renae came to visit me after the 1990 holidays.

Renae flew in on Delta Airlines. I picked her up at the airport and I was very excited to see a familiar face and she was looking fine. We headed for my place, but I told her I had to pick up Aaron from the daycare provider. After picking up Aaron, we made it back to my place. Renae said the place could use a woman's touch and that she could tell that I was a man living alone. We talked about old times and our plans for the future.

Later that evening, after I put little Aaron to bed, Renae and I settled in for the night. I hadn't been with a woman in months and I was excited and horny about having Renae in my bed. I reached over to touch her and she let me get to first base, but then she said there would be no homeruns tonight. I felt like I needed the coldest of showers.

The next day was Saturday and we decided to go to the gym. Renae and Aaron played on the basketball court next to the main court while I was playing. They seem to be getting along pretty good. In between games, I went over and played with them both. Most of the guys knew my situation and they were all looking and wondering. The base is like Peyton Place, where everybody is into whatever is the news of the day. So the idea of me with another woman spread like wildfire. We left the gym and went to Disneyworld, and we had a great time. Aaron loved the Teenage Mutant Ninja Turtles. He used to carry one of the Turtles around with him all the time. When he saw a life-sized turtle, he turned and ran into my arms.

On Sunday, Renae decided she would stay at my place and watch Aaron while I went to the gym. When I arrived, several guys asked who that fine lady was with me yesterday. I told them she was my college sweetheart. I knew I had turned the corner from my past relationship. Renae saved me money for the week she came to visit, because she watched Aaron for three days of the week. On Thursday and Friday, she wanted some down time to get some rest.

While she was at my place, there was one awkward moment. The landlord came over to fix something and he found Renae sleeping. He did not know she was there and I didn't know he was coming over. He did what he had to do and he left. He called me and said there was a woman in my duplex and I told him I knew.

The week went too fast. Friday had come and Renae was headed back to Baltimore. I didn't want to see her leave, but I knew she had to go. We embraced and I kissed her. She off ered to move in with me and I told her no. I had to get over some personal stuff before I could give her 100% of myself. I felt she was too good for that.

Renae and I became even closer after her visit. We talked all the time and she made me feel good. After talking with Renae, I always had this smile on my face. One day my smile was so obvious when I picked up Aaron that the daycare provider asked about it. The other thing that made me smile was the look on Aaron's face when it was time to pick him up.

During this period of my life, I needed him as much as he needed me. As the days passed, the thought of becoming a professional basketball had all but gone. It was time for me to get out of the service and start a new chapter in my life. When my enlistment ended, I had eight weeks of vacation saved up, so I could take as much as two months off before I looked for a new job.

Irene and Sheridan came over to my duplex the day before I was about to drive my U-Haul truck back to Baltimore. The three of us had become very close and we all wanted the best for each other. They wished me well and we parted ways with respect. It was the closure of a nice three-year period of close friendship.

I called Renae the night before and told her I would be on my way in the morning. Renae and I had talked extensively about what I was going to do once I got back to Baltimore. She was in the process of buying a house. She said the relator, who was selling her the house, was trying to get her to go out with him. She told him she was taken. We both decided to give our relationship a try to see if we could pick up where we left off in college and have a go at a long-term relationship. Renae was the only reason I went back to Baltimore. There was nothing in Baltimore for me, other than my family. I liked being out on my own and the satisfaction it gave me to know I was still succeeding, despite some setbacks.

Finally, I arrived in Baltimore on a Tuesday. I had to turn in the truck to U-Haul to get a refund of some of my down payment as a military member separating from the service. Before I could turn the truck in, I went to Shanice's mother's house and dropped off some of her personal things that she had asked me to bring back to Baltimore. Once I did all that, I contacted Renae and she said she already had a storage facility with some of her things in and that I could put my things in there also. The location was close to where my mother lived. Renae was living in an apartment with a girlfriend. Aaron and I stayed with my mother. I had to get use to staying with my mother again. It was different because I had been out on my own, but I thoroughly enjoyed my time there because it gave me a chance to reconnect with my mother and sisters.

After a couple of weeks, Renae secured the house and we collected our things to move in.

 THE WORLD DOESN'T END WHEN IT SEEMS OUR DREAM HAS WANDERED OUT OF SIGHT.

Chapter 7

RESURGENCE

Obstacles don't have to stop you. If you run into a wall, don't turn around and give up. Figure out how to climb it, go through it, or work around it.

~ MICHAEL JORDAN

The first night we spent in the new house was one of the nights of my life, a night I will never forget. Renae, Aaron and I didn't have much when we moved in and we spent the night sleeping on a quilt on the floor in our basement. I had Renae and Aaron in my arms. Our bed set was to be delivered the next day, but this night was as wholesome and endearing as any night ever. Everything was moving along nicely and I was satisfied with the decision I had made. Aaron was in Head Start and I had a good support base around me.

One day Renae came home from working her two jobs and asked me, "What have you been doing?" I said, "Nothing." She went off on a tangent. She said, "I've been working all day and you have been doing nothing." She said her family had been asking what I was doing. I told her to stop right there. I didn't care what her family thought of me. I was there for her and Aaron. I told her what we had would never work unless we were on the same page. I left. How quickly things can change!

I started second guessing my decision to come to Baltimore. I packed my things and took Aaron and went back to my mother's house.

Two weeks passed and Renae and I talked sparingly. One Thursday, after she got off from work, she came over to my mother's house.

Renae came up the stairs to my room and asked if we could talk. She said, "I don't think the disagreement we had was handled the right way." I agreed with her. She asked me to move back in. I told her I was not some deadbeat brother who intended to remain unemployed. I knew how to take care of my responsibilities. I would find a job, and we would be okay. She apologized and told me how much she missed me.

She needed six hundred dollars to help with some bills and she had asked her family but no one could help. I told her she should have asked me. She didn't because I was unemployed. I told her I would take care of it. I asked her to take me to Andrews AFB after she got off work the next day.

The next day was Friday. She came and picked me around 1 PM. We headed for Andrews. I needed to find out from Andrews how to get to military pay. Once inside, I filled out some paperwork and I asked to get an advance on my eight weeks of vacation. I collected the money and handed it over to Renae. We made amends. I moved back in and everything moved along fine.

Renae and I tried relentlessly to set up visitation rights for Shanice. It just never seemed to work out. After Renae and I got into another argument about Shanice, Renae blessed me good and kicked me out again. She said I needed to get my life together and find out what I really wanted. I left again. This time it was only for the weekend. I talked with Renae but she wasn't listening to me. She was at the point where she said, "Don't talk to me unless you are ready to be with me wholeheartedly."

The following Monday, I showed up unannounced. She was working on the house and she had a young man helping her. I would later find out that the young man was interested in being with her. When I showed up, Renae asked what I was doing there. I told her I was back. The young man gathered his things and left. At this point we were really making a go of it. Renae was able to find suitable daycare for Aaron close to the house and we both took turns picking him up. I was able to secure a job with a temporary agency before I received my last check from the military. The temp agency had me working in a warehouse and it was hard labor. We were unloading trailers full of merchandise. Depending on how many trailers I got each day, it was a real workout. Sometimes we would get five or six trailers and it would take all day. Then there were times we would get two trailers and were done early. The supervisor would let us go early, pay us for the day and allow us to go look for another job. He felt none of us were going to stay there long. The warehouse was in Baltimore County, MD and I was able to secure another job around the corner. This job was packing and shelving books. After working both jobs, all I wanted to do was go to sleep once I got home. I would still get in my days of playing basketball on Saturday and Sunday.

 MISSED OPPORTUNITIES AND FADING DREAMS CAN LEAVE US WALLOWING AT THE BOTTOM OF THE PILE, BUT WE MUST KNOW THAT STAYING THERE IS A CHOICE.

Three of us who unloaded the trailers. One day, one of the guys called out to Darrell. He was kind of small in stature. He had already seen that we would be unloading. treadmills. Darrell said, "Hey, I will get up in the top of the trailer and I will push them down to you because I can't lift them." There was something wrong with the treadmills. They had to be unloaded and a pin had to be taken out of them and then they had to be reloaded. The treadmills were at least 150 pounds. We unloaded all three trailers. Lucky for us, the supervisor said we could leave them out on the floor and reload them the next day. I wasn't too happy about what I had in store for me the next day.

There were days when someone called out and I had to do double work. I didn't call out because I needed the money. But that morning, after working hard the previous day, I called the temp agency to say I wasn't going in. The young lady on the phone said, "You are going to get up out of that bed and you are going to go to work." Renae took the phone and said to the lady, "He is not ever coming back to this job and I would like for you to meet Mr. Click." She hung up.

Finding a credible job was becoming a real challenge. I needed to find a job that off ered the same type of benefits as the military. A job with benefits would help me take care of my family better. This was the year 1991. I had been able to get a reserve assignment at The Delaware Air Force Reserves. I attended duty once a month and two weeks during the summer, or anytime I could fit in the two weeks.

In November of 1991 I started driving to Delaware for duty. My first trip was very nice and I enjoyed the new people that I met. I stayed in the dorms that were provided for weekenders, as we were called. I worked in an administrative office located all the way on the other side of the base.

One Sunday, the supervisor let everyone in our office off from work to allow us to beat the traffic. I attended drill in Delaware just once more and that was it for me. I didn't like making the drive. I needed to find something closer.

While I was playing basketball with a friend I went to high school with, he mentioned that he was in the Maryland Air National Guard. I had no idea what that was. He explained it was a military establishment that is generally a state local part of the military. The Air Guard is made up of those who have full time jobs at the base, and the rank structure is the same as the Air Force. He told me the location, and gave me the recruiter's number.

I called and met with the recruiter. He was able to secure a position for me in another field, which was supply. I would have to go away to school to learn the position or learn it through CDC's, which was basically in-house training.

I started attending drill at the MD Air Nat'l Guard in January of 1992. It was very nice not having to make the drive to Delaware. The MD Air Guard was an hour and a half away from where Renae and I lived. This was great because it allowed me to come home instead of staying in the dorms. The dorms weren't bad in Delaware, I just liked the idea of coming home after drill.

My military career in the Air Guard was going along as planned and I enjoyed it. While in the Guard, I met Vernon Crider, who became my best friend in the Guard. Vernon and I hit it off right from the get go. We began attending events together outside of the Guard and every time we were deployed, Vernon and I would room together.

After a few drills, the Guard's supply department started to downsize. The supply commander off ered me a transfer to the Contracting Office. I would have to attend technology school for four weeks. I didn't mind because I needed the money and I hadn't secured a permanent job yet.

When I transferred to the Contracting Office, I met two young ladies, Sgt. Dana Dowell and Sgt. Susan Sowa, who I formed a friendship and a bond with for the next fifteen years. They are my friends to this day and I keep in touch with them as much as I can.

Over the years, Dana, Susan, and I had many conversations together and we saw our kids grow up together. We attended deployments together and I learned so much from them both about the contracting field. Dana was the office supervisor.

For the next fifteen years, I attended schools and deployments to diff erent bases. I obtained Level 7 in the Administrative and Contracting Field. I attended Leadership School for six weeks in Knoxville, Tennessee and was one of a few weekenders to do so.

Usually, the full-time guardsmen attended six weeks of training. When I started at the MD Air National Guard, I began as a Senior Airmen/Buck Sgt. I went on to become a SSgt., a TSgt, and a MSgt. I retired as a SMSgt. I could not have achieved any of this without the help of Dana Dowell, Susan Sowa, Renae Molock and Col. Solomon, who encouraged me to go to leadership school.

 THE PATH OF LIFE MAY NOT ALWAYS TAKE US WHERE WE WANTED TO GO, BUT IT WILL LEAD US WHERE WE NEED TO GO.

Chapter 8
MAKING IT OFFICIAL

Your work is going to fill a large part of your life, and the only way to be truly satisfied is to do what you believe is great work. And the only way to do great work is to love what you do. If you haven't found it yet, keep looking. Don't settle. As with all matters of the heart, you'll know when you find it.

~ STEVE JOBS

When I was still looking for a permanent job, after working at the warehouse, I was able to get a job at a trucking agency. My responsibility was to load trucks and drive the forklifts. The job was evenings from 3 PM to 11 PM. This is what they told me in the interview process.

On my first day at the job, I worked until 11 PM and I was ready to go. The supervisor told me I could not leave yet. I asked why and said I was told to work until 11. He said we all work until the floor is cleared and all the work is completed. I didn't get off until 3 AM that morning. I was pissed. On my way home, I made a conscious decision not to return.

The next day at 2:30 PM, Renae called and asked what I was doing at home and why I hadn't left for work. I told her I quit that job. She was upset that I didn't discuss it with her and didn't think about them before I quit. I told her she and Aaron were the reason I quit. They lied to me about having a set schedule, and such an arrangement would aff ect our family life. My career at the trucking agency ended that day.

I continued to look for work and was becoming more and difficult for Renae to deal with. I had a short fuse and I wasn't my happy jovial self. I wasn't accustomed to being out of work and I always knew my next move or I would prepare for it.

I checked the newspaper one day and found an advertisement for a mail processor at the University of Maryland at Baltimore. I looked over the ad thoroughly and came with benefits and vacation, and it was a State job. The job didn't off er a lot of money, but the benefit package made up for it and it seemed to be what I was looking for. I applied for the job and I was granted an interview, which would prove to be very interesting.

On the day of the interview, I met a man named Mr. Ellsworth Hill. It turned out Mr. Hill knew my father and they had grown up together. I was sure I would get the job with him looking out for me. He decided not to sit in on the interview process because he knew my father, and didn't want to appear biased. That's exactly why I wanted him to sit on the interview board.

After the interview, they said they would get in touch with me. I thought I did very well in the interview and I was confident I had gotten the job. Two weeks passed and I hadn't heard from UMB. Finally, Tom Gazda and said I got the job. I was happy and excited and couldn't wait to tell Renae.

Renae was working for Aramark at Oriole Park at Camden Yards. She had been able to also get me a part-time job with Aramark working on the Club Level. Things were coming together and we were moving forward.

Renae came home from work one day and said, "We need to talk." She was ready to get married. She gave me an ultimatum, well, at least that is how I interpreted it, but she didn't mean it that way (Love you, Renae).

She explained that she could not continue to live under the same roof with me because it was considered fornicating. She thought we were doing well and should make our relationship official. The process moved quickly and her family was concerned. They didn't know me that well, even though Renae and I had been college sweethearts. We both had lived a little before we decided to get married, and that time apart made us appreciate each other even more. We got married on March 29 1992 in a very small church, and much of the family did not attend. It was a small wedding, but it was one of the happiest days of my life.

Leading up to the wedding everyone said I would be the one who would be late for the wedding. It turns out that Renae was the one who was late for the wedding. But when I tell you it was worth the wait, it was worth the wait. When Renae came through the door, she was, and still is, the most beautiful woman I have ever seen. Her smile and her eyes lit up the whole room as she walked down the aisle. Aaron was behind her carrying the ring. For about five minutes, there was no one else in the church except me and her. I was in love with this woman. To this day, I still remember how she looked on our wedding day and it still fills my heart with joy and happiness. I was dressed in black and white. Renae was wearing the prettiest dress you ever did see.

We waited to go on an extended honeymoon because I got the job with the University of Maryland Baltimore and I started April 7, 1992, which was on my birthday. I also got the job with Aramark and I started this job at the end of May 1992. I was working three jobs and it was sometimes tough keeping up with the schedule. When I started working at UMB it was tough at first and I thought, "What the hell have I gotten myself into!" There was so much mail to sort on my first day, way more mail than we use to get in the military. My coworkers had me learn the toughest route right off the bat. I was the new guy and I didn't know any better. They had me on a particular route for six months. I was anxious to learn another route.

When it was time to rotate routes, everyone wanted to switch with me all the time. I always said yes because I didn't know any of the other routes. Once I finally got familiarized with some of the other routes, I realized my coworkers had pulled the wool over my eyes about the other routes. The route I was on was so much tougher than all the other routes, but I toughed it out and made it past my probation period.

After six months, I was informed that the UMB Mail Center was making some cuts and asked if I would like to join the campus security department. Campus Security made less money than the mail center, and I thought Renae wasn't going to like it. But this job had all the benefits I needed to take care of my family. I did not make a lot of money, but the benefits were good. I informed Renae of what was going on and she advised me to look for another job. I told her I wanted to stick it out and see what happened.

As luck would have it, one of the regular employees in the mail center secured another job with the United States Postal Service. This opened the door for me to get a permanent position. I was happy. It is different for a man than it is for a woman when it comes to pride in taking care of their family. I was taught at an early age the responsibilities of taking care of my woman and family. Some men like to run and hide from these responsibilities. I get more satisfaction from knowing I have done the right thing by my wife and my family.

At this point in my life, I was in my late 20s going on 30. I was still playing basketball on a regular basis. My job at UMB allowed me to visit the campus during my lunch break. This was much the same as when I was in the military and was a good situation for me. I got a chance to play basketball at work and then I worked at the baseball stadium in the evening. I was doing reserve duty on the weekends.

Chapter 9

GETTING BACK IN THE GROOVE

Follow your passion, be prepared to work hard and sacrifice, and, above all, don't let anyone limit your dreams.

~ DONOVAN BAILEY

While at UMB, some guys asked if I would like to play intermurals in the evening. I also hooked up with the friends I knew from playing 3 on 3 before I went into the service: Sam, Timmy, and Kevin. We got back together to form Four the Hard Way, our 3 on 3 team.

Each year during the summer, Baltimore had a 3 on 3 tournament that would attract many people for a two-day weekend. My friends and I won this tournament several times. One particular year really stands out. A team had to win four games to win the championship. One game we played was very tightly contested. The team we played in the finals was scouting our team all day on Saturday and again Sunday morning. The whispers were that they had to try and keep the ball out of my hands and force one of the other guys to beat them. We easily won the two games we played on Saturday. The first game we won on Sunday put us in the championship game and we only won by two points.

The Championship game went back and forth and the other team even took the lead by two points. It was the first time we had trailed in any of our games. I was able to tie the game with a two-point shot. It was tied at seventeen. We then scored to take a one-point lead. They then scored on a two-point shot to take the lead by one point. Once again, we scored to tie the game at 19. Then they scored to make it 20 to 19. I made a layup on a spin move to make the game 20 to 20. The first team to 21 would win.

Their defense was to deny me the ball, and it was working. I could not get open to get a good look and they kept leaving Sam open for the shot. Sam drove to the left elbow of the foul line and put up a shot that seemed like it was in the air for 10 seconds. It went in the net and we won the game. We were so excited because this team was good and it was a nice clean game.

The first season at UMB, I played with the guys on my job and we had a nice team. We just didn't have enough to win it all. In my first game, I scored 40 points and we won, but it took a lot of energy to get that win. We went on to have a winning record, but we lost in the playoff s. I was playing a lot, reigniting my passion for playing basketball. I played at lunch time and then again in the evening.

The next season, I was picked up by one of the better teams and we went on to win the intermural championship. It came at a cost. When I got home that evening, Renae was waiting and I could see she was angry. She was sick of babysitting

Aaron while I was out playing basketball until 8pm. I had never seen her that upset. I fired back and told her that instead of being angry, she should find something to do. This is when it all started. Renae decided she liked real estate. She took the course, passed, and received her realtor's license. I was so proud of her. She was moving forward and so was I.

I was training to get promoted in the military and doing CDC course work to get promoted to Technical Sgt. Renae and I discussed moving to another house. I had to go away for military training for four weeks to move up another level in the contracting field.

When I was away, I called Renae almost every night. She would tell me how her day went and how the house hunting was coming. She said it was very frustrating looking for a house without me there. It started to wear on her so much that when she told me about the houses, and I told her what I didn't like, she snapped at me and said I needed to be there. I missed her. I encouraged her to stop stressing. We would eventually find the right house.

When I got back from training, we scheduled a house showing in Rosedale, MD. It was a three-bedroom house with a nice yard with a large hill. It had a nice basement area. After viewing the house, we both decided this was the house for us. We placed a contract on the house and we were awarded our new house. Renae was very happy and when she is happy, I am very happy. I am not a materialistic person and Renae isn't either, but when you work towards something together, it is even more satisfying. We were the first black couple to move into the neighborhood.

We lived on a dead-end street and we liked it because the neighbors knew who lived on the street, and who had no business in the area. After moving to our new house, Renae decided to start a business. She called the business LockSpar Living. This name represents part of my last name (Molock) and part of her maiden last name (Sparks). The success of renting this house was very reassuring, because I didn't want to go into the Landlord business unless I was very comfortable. Renae would always make me feel comfortable before we moved on. Moving on is just what we did.

Renae went to several auctions and acquired several more properties. As we were building up funds, this allowed her the flexibility to purchase more houses without going to auctions. We went out and work on the houses ourselves, with the help of her brother, Robert Sparks. Robert is a gifted carpenter and he helped us to establish the business. The business was progressing and Renae had to get certified for her realtor's license each year. I was still playing basketball and she would sometimes go to the gym with me and watch me play or watch me play intermurals. I had made Master Sgt. and was scheduled to put on Senior Master Sgt. First, I had to go to the Tennessee National Guard Training Center to complete the six-week course to get promoted. This was going to be a long time away from Renae and my duties at the University of MD Baltimore, but it was a chance for me to advance. While in Tennessee, I found myself missing Renae once again.

I met two guys, Brian and Steve. We were all housed in the same dormitory, but we were in diff erent classes. Brian was from Ohio. Steve was from Louisiana. We played basketball together and went to the club together. We would sit in the day room area in the evening. There are several stories about my time in Tennessee, but one stands out more than the others. My friend Brian was the victim of this particular story.

When we first went to the Tennessee training base, on our first day they took us through a series of events and questions to find out who knew what and who would need a little more attention. At the end of the day, Brian just happened to be one of the guys they asked to meet with later that day in the auditorium. We went our separate ways and I told him I would meet with him later that evening.

About seven that evening, we met up again. I asked Brian what they wanted with him. He said they wanted to find out if those called to the auditorium could comprehend. He said they had him there reading stuff like "See the cat run" and "The dog was in the woods." I started laughing. He said it was a bunch of bullshit and a waste of his time. We then had a few drinks and laughed all evening about his ordeal.

The next morning while going to class, I noticed Brian speaking to certain people with just a nod of his head and I asked him what that was all about. He said that was one of the guys who was in the auditorium with him. They had a secret code no one knew about. He then told me his secret. He said he sees dumb people. I asked him where and he said everywhere. We laughed for about an hour.

The training at the Tennessee training site consisted of leadership training that would help us become better supervisors and leaders as we moved further along in our careers. My roommate Bishop was Caucasian and a little younger than me. We had some good conversations in the evening after school. Some evenings I even talked with Bishop's wife when she called and he wasn't there. She would say, "I know he is down at the NCO Club," and she was right. Bishop liked going to the NCO Club.

At the NCO Club, Bishop was well known. And in the morning when I went to class, I heard people talking about him in the halls.

I decided to go to the club one evening and find out what was going on. Bishop was on stage doing karaoke, performing one of Frank Sinatra's songs. He was great! He had the hat on, he had the cigarette in his hand, and he had a drink in his hand. The crowd was eating it up. The people in the club were buying him drinks like crazy. No wonder he liked going there.

He saw me and called me over. The club members started buying me drinks because I was his roommate. It was fun at its best.

Brian and I were also very competitive on the basketball court. I was an older player and he was a little younger than I was. He didn't think I could play ball, but he soon got a lesson in how to play the game of basketball. The thing about basketball is it is a universal sport and can often be a catalyst for making friends anywhere in the world.

We graduated from the Leadership Training. Renae flew down to Tennessee to watch me graduate, and she was very proud of me. It was so nice to see her, because I hadn't seen her for six weeks and it seemed like a year.

When I got back to Baltimore, I felt pretty good about my military status. That experience helped me go on to become a SMSgt.

My average playing weight had always been 185 to 195 pounds. At age I was still actively playing basketball on the UMB Intermural team, but I was about 210 pounds and my game was changing. I could no longer do some of the things I did when I was younger. But I was still a player they had to guard, and I could not be left alone.

Another story I remember was playing against a team that didn't have the talent we had. But in this game they were up for the challenge and in the first half they kept the game very close. I was having a very good game and had twenty points by the end of the first half. I threw a hook shot from half court out of desperation and it went in all nets. But we were only up by ten points at the half.

In the second half, we started to pull away and managed to get the lead to twenty points. At the end of the game, with the clock running out, I shot a three-point shot and it went in all nets again. One of the players on the other team took exception to this and said, "Come on man, you didn't have to shoot that last shot, you guys are already winning by 20 points." I didn't shoot the ball to disrespect the team. I finished with forty-three points.

I am telling this story because I was a mail courier on campus and one day, while completing my route, I ran into the same guy who thought I should not have taken the shot. He said, "Hey, you are that guy who scored forty-three points against us the other night." He then asked forgiveness for his behavior that night. I told him no worries, and wished him luck on his other games. I was making a name for myself as well as my teammates. We were now the team everyone wanted to beat in intermural. Other teams came to our games to scout our team.

YOU DON'T HAVE TO MAKE A PROFESSIONAL TEAM TO MAKE A NAME FOR YOURSELF. IN SPORTS, THERE ARE MANY UNSUNG HEROES WHO MAINTAINED A GOOD REPUTATION IN MANY SPORTS.

A guy from one of the teams we were to play one night asked his teammate, "Which one of the guys on their team do you think we have to worry about the most?" The teammate said, "I 've played with and against the one guy name Pepe. The guy name Jeff you must guard because he is a good three-point shooter. The guy over there that looks like he can barely walk and has an awkward shot, at the end of the night he will have thirty points and 11 to 12 rebounds and you will be looking around saying to yourself where did it come from? He is unassuming, but he is savvy around the basket and he can shoot from anywhere on the court." He was talking about me.

During this period, the Manager of the UMB Mail Center had become unavailable. I saw it as a promotion, but also as an opportunity to make more money. I told Renae about the position and she said go for it. I was apprehensive because I had tried three times before and each time I did not get the position. The final analysis would be, "Could I supervise individuals I had worked alongside of for 16 years?" My current supervisor Mr. Larry Butler told me to throw my hat into the arena. He believed in me, that I could handle the position with no problem. I thought long and hard before I decided to go after the Manager's position, mostly because I had been working alongside my coworkers for sixteen years and I knew their tendencies and their habits. I was also comfortable with my present position, because I could come to work and only have to police myself. But I decided to go for the position. This time around I had the attitude of Morgan Freeman in Shawshank Redemption. Either they were going to hire me for this position or stop wasting my time.

I was interviewed by a panel of four individuals. When I left, I thought the interview went very well, but I wasn't sure I got the position. Larry wanted me to get the position.

A couple of days went by and the suspense was mounting. Then Larry called me to his office and he said, "Moe, you are going to be the new Manager of the UMB Mail Center." I was very happy about the promotion and I couldn't wait to tell Renae. We went out to dinner and I told her I got the Manager's position. She was ecstatic.

 EVERY LESSON, EVERY DIFFICULTY, EVERY PERSON WE ENCOUNTER IN OUR LIFE'S JOURNEY WILL PREPARE US FOR THAT ONE POSITION IN LIFE THAT WILL SEEM TO HAVE BEEN TAILOR MADE FOR US.

Chapter 10

PAST FAILURES, FUTURE SUCCESS

"Success is to be measured—not so much by the position that we have reached in life—as by the obstacles that we have overcome while trying to succeed."

~ BOOKER T. WASHINGTON

I began my tenure as University of Maryland Baltimore Postal Manager in August of 2006 and I am currently the Manager now. At this point in my career, I continued to play basketball, but now I was slowing down and I could see and feel it. I was still a contributing player, but my body was starting to tell me something diff erent. I like to work out, but nothing gave me the satisfaction that basketball did. With basketball, I could talk trash to my opponents, who were now much younger than I am. I now have the title of a Legend. This is what they call me once I come through the door because I can still play and have played so long. Many of the guys I played with and grew up with are no longer playing.

I now have a series of things I do and say on the court while I am playing. If I get a nice pass from one of my teammates, I rub my hand on the side of my shorts because they know the shot is going. Also, I say "That's Too Much Room" when a defensive player is playing off me at about two feet. If you give me that much room, you are at my mercy.

I liked playing ball with the younger guys. It was a lot of fun. I am amazed at how much the game has changed since I was young. The guys are a lot faster and taller, but they cannot shoot the basketball the way we did when we were younger. I play a real basic game now. I shoot from long distance on the perimeter and I post up down low and use a traditional hook shot as my primary weapon.

At this point, as the Postal Manager for UMB, I am responsible for several couriers and we are responsible for the mail of seven thousand individuals. We service 200 stops on campus. The personnel I manage is a good group, and we sort and deliver every piece of mail we receive each day. This includes mail that is to be signed for and internal mail that slows through the campus. We are partners with the University of Maryland Hospital Mailroom and both departments support each other to the utmost. The UMB Mail Center continues to do an exceptional job across the campus. We are constantly getting good reviews from the campus customers. My supervisor, Lawrence Butler, is a great supervisor. He allows me to run the mail center as I see fit. He advises me on many matters. At the end of our discussions, he would say,

"That's my advice, but it is your decision." I like my job and I have always been a customer service oriented person.

Basketball taught me how to work hard and be consistent with my everyday duties. I once played basketball every day, and if I could I would still play every day. I have a real love for the game that has given me so much in the way of physical health, recognition, friends, the ability to travel around, and a place to get away from the everyday stress of life itself. The game is played all over the world and it is constantly growing. It is a game that is now played globally by men and women. I like to watch the women play, because they play a more thinking game than the men.

Millions of kids and young men play all types of sports all over the world. Millions aspire to become professional athletes in one of those sports. But we must understand that each professional sport consists of one to maybe five hundred players. And if we do the math, the chances of becoming a professional athlete are very slim.

Today, we must be in a great situation to become a professional. We must have a great support group willing buy into our goal and what we are trying to accomplish for ourselves and, in many cases, our family. If a family has an athlete they think has a good shot at becoming a professional, they may have to make many sacrifices for this to happen. In my case, I didn't have that one person who would guide me on the route I needed to take.

One defining moment in my life was when I sat in the office with my high school basketball coach and he said. "I have three scholarships. I don't have four. I would sure like to give you one, but there are three individuals who I have already picked." I only played one year of high school basketball. In that moment, I was just happy he considered me and that I was on the team.

As I look back now, I needed someone who could have helped me talk with a coach or advise me on my next move. My point is this, there are millions of athletes trying to become professionals who need to be prepared if it doesn't happen. Some will say it didn't happen because they didn't give it their all. But if we are a contributing member to the livelihood of our family, how can we give it our all? Many athletes throw themselves into the idea that becoming a professional athlete is their only option. They must realize that this is not true. Becoming a professional athlete is "Not the Only Ticket." One can still become successful and maybe even more successful than if they were a professional athlete. What happens to these individuals if it doesn't happen for them and the crowd is no longer cheering their names? These athletes sometimes live in obscurity. This is because it was all or nothing and there was no backup plan. Some of our best athletes are walking the streets still talking of what could have been. They turn to drugs or work mediocre jobs to make ends meet.

My message is this: You can still be successful. I spared no details in telling you my story, and you may not have easily seen the relevance of some of the things I have shared, but they are fragments of the whole, pieces of the puzzle that painted the full picture.

Success is not defined by how much money you make or how many degrees or cars or houses you may have. Success is defined by how you feel about who you are. Can you live with the person you are? All of us have at some point been victims of failed opportunities or a once in a lifetime chance we watched slip away from us. We must pick ourselves up and determine our self-worth. Our value is not determined by our circumstances, bad choices, missed opportunities, or other people's opinion of us. If you don't become a professional athlete, then find something else you like to do. Our life and future is our responsibility and it hangs on the day-to-day choices we make.

I never thought my wife and I would get into the business of renting houses, but it happened. I resolved in my mind that working my job at UMB and my wife working her job at Union Memorial, we would live a comfortable life.

If you work at McDonald's or if you are a trash collector, then be the best McDonald's worker ever. Be the best trash collector ever. Your success will be what you make of it. In my case, at the end of the day, the things I am most proud of are that I have been a good husband and a good father. I have made lots of friends. I love my family.

At this point in my life, I am proud of all my accomplishments. I am proud that our son Aaron Louis Molock is successful. My only goal now is to spend the rest my days enjoying my time with Renae Molock. She said to me one evening that I make her feel safe. This is probably the best compliment ever.

One final thought. My mother passed away in April 2009. I think the biggest responsibility of any son is to lessen the worry of their parents. Before my mother passed away, I lived with the thought that my mother could go to sleep at night knowing that her son was not out in the streets doing the wrong thing or caught up in some mess.

Being a professional athlete sounds great, but I am comfortable with who I am. Call it missed opportunities, or a failure on my part to maximize my own potential, but it just never happened for me, and it wasn't the end of the world. I made a new world.

I would like to add that my story isn't over. My story is still being written and with each day there comes another challenge. I don't know exactly where my next endeavor will come from, and my body of work speaks for itself. You never know what life is going to throw at you each day, but whatever it is, you have the capacity and potential to overcome.

I have resolved that as long as I have my wife at my side, it will be well.

 AT THE END OF THE DAY, YOUR LIFE IS WHAT YOU MAKE IT TO BE.